STATE ASSESSMENT SYSTEMS
Exploring Best Practices and Innovations

Summary of Two Workshops

Alexandra Beatty, *Rapporteur*

Committee on Best Practices for State Assessment Systems:
Improving Assessment While Revisiting Standards

Center for Education

Division of Behavioral and Social Sciences and Education

NATIONAL RESEARCH COUNCIL
OF THE NATIONAL ACADEMIES

THE NATIONAL ACADEMIES PRESS
Washington, D.C.
www.nap.edu

THE NATIONAL ACADEMIES PRESS 500 Fifth Street, N.W. Washington, DC 20001

This study was supported by a contract between the National Academy of Sciences and the James B. Hunt, Jr. Institute for Educational Leadership and Policy, with additional support from the Bill & Melinda Gates Foundation and the Stupski Foundation. Any opinions, findings, conclusions, or recommendations expressed in this publication are those of the author(s) and do not necessarily reflect the views of the organizations or agencies that provided support for the project.

International Standard Book Number-13: 978-0-309-16176-3
International Standard Book Number-10: 0-309-16176-2

Additional copies of this report are available from the National Academies Press, 500 Fifth Street, N.W., Lockbox 285, Washington, DC 20055; (800) 624-6242 or (202) 334-3313 (in the Washington metropolitan area); Internet, http://www.nap.edu.

Printed in the United States of America

Suggested citation: National Research Council. (2010). *State Assessment Systems: Exploring Best Practices and Innovations: Summary of Two Workshops.* Alexandra Beatty, Rapporteur. Committee on Best Practices for State Assessment Systems: Improving Assessment While Revisiting Standards. Center for Education, Division of Behavioral and Social Sciences and Education. Washington, DC: The National Academies Press.

THE NATIONAL ACADEMIES
Advisers to the Nation on Science, Engineering, and Medicine

The **National Academy of Sciences** is a private, nonprofit, self-perpetuating society of distinguished scholars engaged in scientific and engineering research, dedicated to the furtherance of science and technology and to their use for the general welfare. Upon the authority of the charter granted to it by the Congress in 1863, the Academy has a mandate that requires it to advise the federal government on scientific and technical matters. Dr. Ralph J. Cicerone is president of the National Academy of Sciences.

The **National Academy of Engineering** was established in 1964, under the charter of the National Academy of Sciences, as a parallel organization of outstanding engineers. It is autonomous in its administration and in the selection of its members, sharing with the National Academy of Sciences the responsibility for advising the federal government. The National Academy of Engineering also sponsors engineering programs aimed at meeting national needs, encourages education and research, and recognizes the superior achievements of engineers. Dr. Charles M. Vest is president of the National Academy of Engineering.

The **Institute of Medicine** was established in 1970 by the National Academy of Sciences to secure the services of eminent members of appropriate professions in the examination of policy matters pertaining to the health of the public. The Institute acts under the responsibility given to the National Academy of Sciences by its congressional charter to be an adviser to the federal government and, upon its own initiative, to identify issues of medical care, research, and education. Dr. Harvey V. Fineberg is president of the Institute of Medicine.

The **National Research Council** was organized by the National Academy of Sciences in 1916 to associate the broad community of science and technology with the Academy's purposes of furthering knowledge and advising the federal government. Functioning in accordance with general policies determined by the Academy, the Council has become the principal operating agency of both the National Academy of Sciences and the National Academy of Engineering in providing services to the government, the public, and the scientific and engineering communities. The Council is administered jointly by both Academies and the Institute of Medicine. Dr. Ralph J. Cicerone and Dr. Charles M. Vest are chair and vice chair, respectively, of the National Research Council.

www.national-academies.org

COMMITTEE ON BEST PRACTICES FOR
STATE ASSESSMENT SYSTEMS:
IMPROVING ASSESSMENT WHILE REVISITING STANDARDS

Diana Pullin (*Chair*), Lynch School of Education, Boston College
Joan Herman, National Center for Research on Evaluation, Standards, and Student Testing, University of California, Los Angeles
Scott Marion, Center for Assessment, National Center for the Improvement of Educational Assessment, Dover, NH
Dirk Mattson, Research and Assessment Division, Minnesota Department of Education
Rebecca Maynard, Graduate School of Education, University of Pennsylvania
Mark Wilson, Graduate School of Education, University of California, Berkeley

Judith A. Koenig, *Study Director*
Stuart Elliott, *Director, Board on Testing and Assessment*
Alexandra Beatty, *Senior Program Officer*
Kelly Duncan, *Senior Project Assistant*
Kelly Iverson, *Project Assistant*
Rose Neugroschel, *Research Assistant*

Preface

The idea that states might pool their resources and sign on to a common set of education standards has gone from a speculative concept to an emerging reality. Forty-eight states have now signed on to the "common core initiative." States are also responding to the opportunity to compete for significant federal education funds through the Race to the Top Assessment Program, which focuses on improvements to standards and assessments.

Even before these recent developments, the context for decisions about assessment and accountability was shifting as federal and state policy makers began to take stock of the effects of the No Child Left Behind law and to consider possible changes to it. At the same time, researchers—and a few states—have explored approaches to measuring student learning that are based on theoretical models distinctly different from those that have traditionally been used in most state programs. Overall, states are reviewing their approaches to assessment and the role it can and should play in a standards-based accountability system in a complex environment of practical, political, theoretical, and technical questions.

With funding from the James B. Hunt, Jr. Institute for Educational Leadership and Policy, the Bill & Melinda Gates Foundation, and the Stupski Foundation, the National Research Council (NRC) planned two workshops designed to explore some of the possibilities for state assessment systems. Their goal was to pull together data and perspectives on current assessment and accountability systems and on innovative assessment approaches to assist educators and policy makers. The Committee on Best Practices for State Assessment Systems planned the two workshops. The first workshop, held in December

2009, focused on lessons to be drawn from past experiences with innovative assessments, technical challenges, and the opportunities presented by the current common standards movement. The second workshop, held in April 2010, provided a more detailed look at possibilities for developing coherent assessment systems that incorporate innovative approaches. This report describes the presentations and discussions from both workshops. The agendas for the two workshops are in Appendix A; the lists of participants are in Appendix B. The background papers and videotapes of each workshop are posted on the NRC website: http://www7.nationalacademies.org/bota/Best_Practices_Homepage. html [accessed September 2010].

These two workshops were designed to build on two previous ones that examined the possibilities for and questions about common standards for K-12 education. Although a separate committee was responsible for those workshops (reported in National Research Council, 2008), we hope that the body of information produced by all of these workshops provide useful guidance for policy makers in a very fast-changing educational context. More broadly, we hope that the research and perspectives presented in this volume contribute to thoughtful deliberation about longer-term questions and goals for education.

Many people contributed to the success of the two workshops. We first thank the sponsors for their support of this work, the James B. Hunt, Jr. Institute for Educational Leadership and Policy, the Bill & Melinda Gates Foundation, and the Stupski Foundation. We particularly thank Judith Rizzo and Stephanie Dean of the Hunt Institute for their commitment to and assistance with the committee's organization of the workshops.

The committee also thanks the scholars who wrote papers and made presentations at the workshops. For the first workshop, we thank: Steve Ferrara, CTB McGraw-Hill; Margaret Goertz, University of Pennsylvania; Brian Gong, National Center for the Improvement of Educational Assessment; Ron Hambleton, University of Massachusetts, Amherst; Laura Hamilton, RAND; Joe Krajcik, University of Michigan; Stephen Lazer, Educational Testing Service; Lorraine McDonnell, University of California, Santa Barbara; Lorrie Shepard, University of Colorado; Brian Stecher, RAND; Shawn Stevens, University of Michigan; Laurie Wise, HumRRO; and Rebecca Zwick, Educational Testing Service and the University of California, Santa Barbara.

For the second workshop, we thank: Tony Alpert, Oregon Department of Education; Randy Bennett, Educational Testing Service; Peg Cagle, Los Angeles Unified School District, California Teachers Advisory Council; Linda Darling-Hammond, Stanford University; Margaret Heritage, National Center for Research on Evaluation, Standards, and Student Testing, University of California, Los Angeles; Karin Hess, National Center for the Improvement of Educational Assessment; Robert Linquanti, WestEd; Wendy Pickett, Delaware Department of Education; Ed Roeber, Michigan State University; Roy Romer, College Board; Deborah Sigman, California Department of Education; Teri Siskind, South Carolina Department of Education; Martha Thurlow, National Center on Education Outcomes; Marc Tucker, National Center for Education and the Economy; Joe Wilhoft, Washington State Department of Education; Gene Wilhoit, Council of Chief State School Officers; Laurie Wise, HumRRO; and Rebecca Zwick, Educational Testing Service and the University of California, Santa Barbara.

We are also grateful to senior staff members of the NRC's Division of Behavioral and Social Sciences and Education who helped to move this project forward. Michael Feuer, executive director, and Patricia Morison, associate executive director and acting director of the Center for Education, provided support and guidance at key stages in this project. The committee also thanks the NRC staff who worked directly on this project: Kelly Duncan, senior project assistant; Kelly Iverson, senior project assistant; and Rose Neugroschel, research assistant, all with the Board on Testing and Assessment (BOTA), provided deft organizational skills and careful attention to detail that helped to ensure the success of both workshops. We are especially grateful to Judy Koenig, staff director for this workshop project, who played an invaluable role in organizing an informative set of papers and presentations. Judy's wisdom and skills made certain that the workshops would be a useful contribution to the public discourse on these important topics. We are also grateful to Stuart Elliott, BOTA director, and Alix Beatty, BOTA senior program officer, for their contributions in formulating the design of each workshop and making them both a reality. We particularly wish to recognize Alix Beatty for her superb writing skills and ability to translate workshop presentations and discussions into a coherent, readable report.

Finally, as chair of the committee, I thank the committee members for their dedication and outstanding contributions to this project. They gave generously of their time in planning the workshops and participated actively in workshop presentations and discussions. Their varied experiences and perspectives contributed immeasurably to the success of the project and made them a delightful set of colleagues for this work.

This report has been reviewed in draft form by individuals chosen for their diverse perspectives and technical expertise, in accordance with procedures approved by the NRC's Report Review Committee. The purpose of this independent review is to provide candid and critical comments that will assist the institution in making its published report as sound as possible and to ensure that the report meets institutional standards for objectivity, evidence, and responsiveness to the charge. The review comments and draft manuscript remain confidential to protect the integrity of the process. We thank the following individuals for their review of this report: Ken Draut, Office of Assessment and Accountability, Kentucky Department of Education; Robert L. Linn, Department of Education, University of Colorado; Carissa Miller, Assessment Division, Idaho State Department of Education; John P. Poggio, Department of Psychology and Research in Education, University of Kansas; and David F. Shaffer, The Nelson A. Rockefeller Institute of Government, Albany, NY.

Although the reviewers listed above provided many constructive comments and suggestions, they were not asked to endorse the content of the report, nor did they see the final draft of the report before its release. The review of this report was overseen by Edward H. Haertel of the School of Education of Stanford University. Appointed by the NRC, he was responsible for making certain that an independent examination of this report was carried out in accordance with institutional procedures and that all review comments were carefully considered. Responsibility for the final content of this report rests entirely with the author and the institution.

Diana Pullin, *Chair*
Committee on Best Practices for State Assessment Systems:
Improving Assessment While Revisiting Standards

Contents

1   INTRODUCTION   1
    Context, 4
        Changes in Tests, 4
        Interim Assessments, 6
        Multiple Purposes for Assessment, 7
    The Current System, 9
        Strengths, 9
        Weaknesses, 10
        Challenges, 11

2   IMPROVING ASSESSMENTS—QUESTIONS AND
    POSSIBILITIES   15
    Standards for Better Instruction and Learning: An Example, 15
    Assessments for Better Instruction and Learning: An Example, 21
    Innovations and Technical Challenges, 27
    Looking Forward, 31

3   RECENT INNOVATIVE ASSESSMENTS   33
    Looking Back, 34
        Vermont, 34
        Kentucky, 35
        Maryland, 36
        Washington, 36
        California, 37

NAEP Higher-Order Thinking Skills Assessment Pilot, 37
Lessons from the Past, 38
Current Innovations, 38
Performance Assessment, 39
Portfolios, 40
Technology-Supported Assessment, 40

4   POLITICAL EXPERIENCES AND CONSIDERATIONS   43
Maryland, 43
Kentucky, 45
Minnesota, 47
Strategic Implications, 48

5   COHERENT ASSESSMENT SYSTEMS   51
Characteristics of a Coherent System, 52
Perspectives on Implementation, 54
The Policy Process, 54
Curriculum-Embedded Assessments, 57
Computer-Based Testing, 59
Board Examination Systems, 62

6   OPPORTUNITIES FOR BETTER ASSESSMENT   65
Improvement Targets, 65
Cost Savings, 66
Improved Cognitive Analysis, 69
Implications for Special Populations, 70
English Language Learners, 71
Students with Disabilities, 75
Technology, 77
State Perspectives, 80

7   MAKING USE OF ASSESSMENT INFORMATION   83
Using Assessments to Guide Instruction, 83
Supporting Teachers, 85
Practitioners' Perspectives, 89
Aggregating Information from Different Sources, 91

8   CHALLENGES OF DEVELOPING NEW ASSESSMENTS   95
Technically Sound Innovative Assessments, 95
Cross-State Comparisons, 97
Perspectives: Past and Future, 100

9   RESEARCH NEEDS   105
      Theory and Goals, 105
      Research Priorities, 109

REFERENCES   113

APPENDIXES

A   Workshop Agendas   121
B   Workshop Participants   133

1

Introduction

Educators and policy makers in the United States have relied on tests to measure educational progress for more than 150 years, and have used the results for many purposes. During the 20th century, technical advances, such as machines for automatic scoring and computer-based scoring and reporting, have supported the nation's states in a growing reliance on standardized tests for statewide accountability. The history of state assessments has been eventful. Education officials have developed their own assessments, have purchased ready-made assessments produced by private companies and nonprofit organizations, and have collaborated to share the task of test development. They have tried minimum competency testing, portfolios, multiple-choice items, brief and extended constructed-response items, and more. They have contended with concerns about student privacy, test content, and equity—and they have responded to calls for tests to answer many kinds of questions about public education and literacy, international comparisons, accountability, and even property values.

State assessment data have been cited as evidence for claims about many achievements of public education, and the tests have also been blamed for significant failings. Most recently, the implementation of the No Child Left Behind (NCLB) Act of 2001 has had major effects on public education: some of those effects were intended and some were not; some have been positive and some have been problematic.

States are now considering whether to adopt the "common core" academic standards that were developed under the leadership of the National Governors Association and the Council of Chief State School Officers, and they are competing for federal dollars from the U.S. Department of Education's Race to the Top initiative.[1] Both of these activities are intended to help make educational standards clearer and more concise and to set higher standards for students. As standards come under new scrutiny, so, too, do the assessments that measure their results: for example, to be eligible for Race to the Top funds, a state must adopt internationally benchmarked standards and also "demonstrate a commitment to improving the quality of its assessments" (U.S. Department of Education, 2009).

The goal for the two workshops documented in this report was to collect information and perspectives on assessment to help state officials and others as they review current assessment practices and consider improvements. In organizing the workshops, the Committee on Best Practices for State Assessment Systems identified four sets of questions for consideration:

1. How do the different existing tests that have been or could be used to make comparisons across states—such as the National Assessment of Educational Progress (NAEP), the advanced placement (AP) tests, the SAT Reasoning Test (SAT, formerly, the Scholastic Aptitude Test), the ACT (formerly, American College Testing), and the Programme for International Student Assessment (PISA)—compare with each other and with the existing state tests and their associated content and performance standards? What implications do the similarities and differences across these tests have for the state comparisons that they can be used to make?

2. How could current procedures for developing content and performance standards be changed to allow benchmarking to measures and predictions of college and career readiness and also promote the development of a small set of clear standards? What options are there for constructing tests that measure readiness with respect to academic skills? Are there options for assessing "21st century" or "soft" skills that could provide a more robust assessment of readiness than a focus on academic skills alone?

3. What does research suggest about best practices in running a state assessment system and using the assessment results from that system to improve instruction? How does this compare to current state capacity and practices? How might assessment in the context of revised standards be designed to move state practices to more closely resemble best practices?

---

[1]The Race to the Top initiative is a pool of federal money set aside for discretionary grants. States are competing to receive the grants on the basis of their success in four areas: standards and assessments, data systems, improving the teacher work force, and improving the lowest-achieving schools (see http://www2.ed.gov/programs/racetothetop/index.html [accessed March 2010]).

4. How could assessments that are constructed for revised standards be used for accountability? Are there important differences in the use of assessments for accountability if those assessments are based on standards that are (1) shared in common across states, (2) designed to be fewer and clearer, or (3) focused on higher levels of performance?

This was an ambitious agenda and the committee recognized that the workshop series did not allow time for a comprehensive examination of all of these questions. For the first workshop, held in December 2009, the committee focused on lessons to be drawn both from the current status of assessment and accountability programs and the results of past innovation efforts. The second workshop, held in April 2010, explored prospects for implementing coherent assessment systems that can markedly improve learning for all students. This report describes the presentations and discussion from both workshops.[2]

The rest of this chapter describes current approaches to assessment in the United States and some of the recent developments that have shaped them. Chapter 2 explores possibilities for changing the status quo by changing both standards and assessments with the goal of improving instruction and learning. Chapter 3 examines practical and political lessons from past and current efforts to implement innovative assessment approaches, and Chapter 4 focuses on the political considerations that have affected innovative assessment programs. Chapter 5 examines the concept of coherent assessment systems in depth, and Chapter 6 explores several specific targets of opportunity. Chapter 7 focuses on the ways in which richer assessment data could be interpreted and used, and Chapter 8 examines some of the technical challenges of meeting the ambitious goals for innovative assessment. The final chapter offers some of the participants' concluding thoughts and discusses the research needed to support states' efforts to make optimal use of assessments and to pursue innovation in assessment design and implementation.

Many of the sessions at the two workshops delved fairly deeply into technical issues and the practical aspects of developing and running a state assessment system, although the committee's broader goal was to raise provocative questions about the fundamental roles that assessment and accountability play in promoting high-quality teaching and learning to rigorous content and performance standards. In particular, the committee hoped to focus attention on the significant potential that recent research in the learning sciences has to reframe both approaches to assessment and expectations for what assessments can contribute.

---

[2]Because this report synthesizes information from both workshops, it supercedes the report on the first workshop (National Research Council, 2010).

CONTEXT

Standards-based accountability is a widely accepted framework for public education. Every state now has education standards, although the current array of accountability approaches is characterized by significant variation, as Diana Pullin noted. Content and performance standards range widely in rigor, as does the implementation of test-based accountability (see National Research Council, 2008). By design, assessments play a key role in standards-based accountability, and because standards are not working exactly as they were intended to, Pullin suggested, "assessments can be more powerful in driving what happens in schools than standards themselves." Recent research has indicated that the influence of assessments on curriculum and instruction has increased since 2001, when NCLB was passed, and that tests themselves have changed in significant ways (see, e.g., Jennings and Rentner, 2006; McMurrer, 2007; Lai and Waltman, 2008; Sunderman, 2008). Several presenters provided perspectives on the history and current status of assessment and accountability systems.

The idea that assessments should be used to evaluate not only individual students' progress, but also the quality of instruction and the performance of educators more generally, is one with longstanding roots, Joan Herman noted. Edward Thorndike, who published pioneering books on educational measurement in the first decades of the 20th century, viewed his work as useful in part because it would provide principals and teachers with a tool for improving student learning. Ralph Tyler, known for innovative work in educational evaluation in the 1940s, posed the idea that objectives ought to drive curriculum and instruction and that new kinds of assessments (beyond paper-and-pencil tests) were needed to transform learning and the nature of educational programs. Other contributions to thinking about evaluation include Benjamin Bloom's 1956 taxonomy of educational objectives, the development of criterion-referenced testing in the 1950s, mastery learning in the 1960s and 1970s, minimum competency testing in the 1970s and 1980s, and performance assessment in the 1990s. All of these, Herman suggested, have been good ideas, but they have not had the effects that had been hoped for.

Changes in Tests

Most recently, as Scott Marion detailed, NCLB has had a very clear impact on many aspects of the system. Prior to 2002, for example, states were required to test at one grade each in the elementary, middle, and high school years. NCLB required testing in grades 3 through 8 as well as in high school. Marion argued that this increased testing resulted in improvements in state standards. The new requirement compelled states to define coherent content standards by grade level, rather than by grade span, and to articulate more precisely what the performance standards should be for each grade. Testing at every grade has also opened up new possibilities for measuring student achievement over time, such as value-added modeling.[3]

The design of states' tests has also been affected, most notably in a dramatic reduction in the use of matrix sampling designs because they do not provide data on individual students. For a long time, many test designers used matrix sampling to produce data about the learning of large groups of students (such as all children in a single grade) across a broad domain. With this sampling approach, tests are designed so that no one student answers every question (which would require too much testing time for complete coverage), but, taken together, different students' responses to different questions support inferences about how well the group as a whole has learned each aspect of the domain tested. One advantage of matrix sampling is that each student takes fewer test items—because student-level scores are not produced—which allowed developers to include more complex item types. This approach makes it possible to better assess a broad academic domain because the inclusion of more complex item types is likely to yield more generalizable inferences about students' knowledge and skills. However, reporting individual student scores on matrix-samples content is problematic because different students have responded to different questions. Thus, because states are required under NCLB to report results for individual students, matrix sampling is much less commonly used than it had been.

The types of test questions commonly used have also changed, Marion observed, with developers relying far less on complex performance assessments and more on multiple-choice items. He cited evidence from the Government Accounting Office (2009) that the balance between multiple-choice and open-ended items (a category that includes short constructed-response items) has shifted significantly in favor of the multiple-choice format as states have responded to the NCLB requirements. Many states still use items that could be described as open ended, but use of this term disguises important differences between a short constructed-response item worth a few points and an extended, complex performance task that contributes significantly to the overall score. To illustrate the difference, he showed sample items—a four-page task from a 1996 Connecticut test that called for group collaboration and included 16 pages of source materials, contrasted with mathematics items from a 2009 Massachusetts test that asked students to measure an angle and record their result or to construct a math problem and solve it.

Marion was not suggesting that the shorter items—or others like them—are necessarily of inferior quality. Nevertheless, he views this shift as reflecting an increased focus on breadth at the expense of depth. The nature of state assessments under NCLB signals that the most important goal for teachers is

---

[3]"Value-added modeling" is statistical analysis in which student data that are collected over time are used to measure the effects of teachers or schools on student learning.

to ensure that students have an opportunity to learn a broad array of content and skills, even if the coverage is superficial. It is important to ask, if this is the case, whether the types of processes students use to solve multiple-choice items are truly the basis for the 21st century "college- and work-ready" skills that policy makers stress. For example, Marion pointed out, the 1996 Connecticut extended item begins by asking the students to break into small groups and discuss their approach to the task—a challenge much closer to what is expected in many kinds of work than those that are posed by most test items.

States have also changed their approaches to high school testing, though the situation is still in flux. There has been a modest increase in the number of states using end-of-course examinations (given whenever students complete a particular course)—instead of survey tests that all students take at a certain point (such as at the end of particular grades). A few states have begun using college entrance tests as part of their graduation requirements.

Interim Assessments

Another development, discussed by Margaret Goertz, has been a marked increase in the use of interim assessments, particularly at the district level. These assessments measure students' knowledge of the same broad curricular goals that are measured in annual large-scale assessments, but they are given more frequently and are designed to give teachers more data on student performance to use for instructional planning. Interim assessments are often explicitly designed to mimic the format and coverage of state tests. They may be used not only to guide instruction, but also to predict student performance on summative state assessments, to provide data on a program or approach, or to provide diagnostic information about a particular student. Researchers stress the distinction between interim assessments and formative assessments, however, because the latter are typically embedded in instructional activities and may not even be recognizable as assessments by students (Perie and Gong, 2007).[4]

Districts have vastly increased their use of interim assessments in the past 10 years, Goertz noted (see Stecher et al., 2008), and draft guidelines for the Race to the Top initiative encouraged school districts to develop formative or interim assessments as part of comprehensive state assessment systems. However, there have been very few studies of how interim assessments are actually used by individual teachers in classrooms, by principals, and by districts, or of

---

[4]Formative assessments are those designed primarily to provide information that students can use to understand the progress of their learning and that teachers can use to identify areas in which students need additional work. Formative assessments are commonly contrasted with summative assessments, those designed to measure the knowledge and skills students have attained by a particular time, usually after the instruction is complete, for the purpose of reporting on progress. Interim assessments are assessments, which may be formative or summative, that are given at intervals to monitor student progress.

their effects on student achievement, perhaps in part because these are relatively new tools. Moreover, Goertz pointed out, many of the studies that are cited in their favor were actually focused on formative assessments. Moreover, she said, studies are needed to provide technical and other validity evidence to support inferences made from interim assessments.

In surveys, teachers have reported that the results of interim assessments helped them monitor student progress and identify skill gaps for their students and led them to modify curriculum and instruction (Clune and White, 2008; Stecher et al., 2008; Christman et al., 2009). Goertz noted that a study of how teachers used curriculum-based interim assessments in elementary mathematics in two districts showed that teachers did use the data to identify weak areas or struggling students and to make instructional decisions (Goertz, Olah, and Riggan, 2009). The study also showed that teachers varied in their capacity to interpret interim assessment data and to use it to modify their teaching. The study also found that few of the items in the interim assessments provided information that teachers could readily use, and few actually changed their practice even as they retaught material that was flagged by the assessment results. For example, many teachers focused on procedural rather than conceptual sources of error.

Marion noted that the limited research available provides little guidance for developing specifications for interim assessments or for support and training that would help teachers use them to improve student learning. There is tremendous variability in the assessments used in this way, and there is essentially no oversight of their quality, he noted. He suggested that interim assessments provide fast results and seem to offer jurisdictions eager to respond to the accountability imperative in an easy way to raise test scores.

Multiple Purposes for Assessment

Another significant change, Goertz pointed out, is that as demands on state-level assessments have increased in a time of tight assessment budgets, tests are increasingly being used for a number of different purposes. Table 1-1 shows some common testing purposes by goal and by the focus of the information collected. In practice, the uses may overlap, but the table illustrates the complexity of the role that assessments play.

To clarify the implications of putting a single test to multiple uses, Goertz highlighted the design characteristics that are most important for two of these uses, informing instruction and learning and external accountability. For informing instruction and learning, a test should be designed to provide teachers with information about student learning on an ongoing basis, which they can easily interpret and use to improve their instruction. For this purpose, an assessment needs to provide information that is directly relevant to classroom instruction and is available soon after the assessment is given. Ideally, this kind of assess-

TABLE 1-1 Uses of Assessment

Use	Student	Teacher	School
Diagnosis	Instructional decisions; placement; allocation of educational services	Professional development and support	Resource allocation; technical assistance
Inform Teaching and Leaning		Focus, align, redirect content; instructional strategies	Instructional focus, align curriculum to skills or content; school improvement and planning
Evaluation	Certification of individual achievement	Teacher preparation programs; teacher pay	Program evaluation
Public Reporting	Transcripts		Parent or community action
External Accountability	Promotion; high school graduation	Renewal; tenure; pay	Sanctions and rewards

SOURCE: Goertz (2009, p. 3).

ment would provide continuous information: if it is embedded in instruction it can provide continuous feedback. For this purpose, statistical reliability is not as important as relevance and timeliness. In contrast, when test data are to be used for external accountability, the assumption is that information about performance will motivate educators to teach well and students to perform to high standards. Therefore, incentives and sanctions based on test results are often used to stimulate action, which means that the tests have stakes for both students and educators. So, when accountability is the goal, several test characteristics are of critical importance: alignment of test questions to standards; standardization of the content, test administration, and scoring to support fair comparisons; and the fairness, validity, and reliability of the test itself.

The tension between these two purposes is at the heart of many of the problems that states have faced with their assessment programs, and it is a key challenge for policy makers to consider as they weigh improvements to accountability systems.

The growing tendency to use assessments for multiple purposes may be explained in part by the loss of assessment staff in a time of tight education budgets. Marion reported that most states have seen an approximately three-fold increase in testing requirements without a corresponding increase in personnel (Government Accounting Office, 2003; Toch, 2006). As a result, many states have moved from internal test design and development to outside vendors, and, he suggested, remaining staff have less time to work with vendors and to think about innovative approaches to testing.

A number of other factors help explain recent changes in the system, Marion suggested. NCLB required rapid results, and the "adequate yearly progress" formula put a premium on a "head-counting" methodology (measuring how many students meet a particular benchmark by a particular time), rather than considering broader questions about how well students are learning. However, the law did not, in his view, provide adequate financial support for ongoing operational costs. He also said that there has been insufficient oversight of technical quality, so that the validity of particular assessments for particular purposes has received inadequate attention. Marion also noted that because results for multiple-choice and open-ended items are well correlated, many people mistakenly believe that this is evidence that they are interchangeable. An era of tight funding has made it easy for policy makers to conclude that open-ended items and other innovative approaches are not worth their higher cost, he said, without necessarily understanding that such assessment methods make it possible to assess skills and content that cannot be assessed with multiple-choice items.

THE CURRENT SYSTEM

This outline of some of the important recent changes in assessment systems provided the foundation for a discussion of strengths and weaknesses of the current system and targets for improvement. Goertz and Marion presented very similar messages, which were seconded by discussant Joan Herman.

Strengths

Attention to Traditionally Underserved Student Populations Including all students in assessments—to ensure that schools, districts, and states are accountable for their results with every group—was a principal goal of NCLB. As a result, although much work still needs to be done, assessment experts have made important progress in addressing the psychometric challenges of testing students with disabilities and English language learners. Progress has been made in understanding the validity of assessments for both of these groups, which are themselves very heterogeneous. Test designers have paid attention to the challenges of more explicitly specifying the constructs to be measured and removing construct irrelevant variance from test items (e.g., by reducing the reading burden in tests of mathematics so that the measure of students' mathematics skills will not be distorted by reading disabilities). As policy makers and psychometricians have worked to strike an appropriate balance between standardization and technical quality, more assessments are available to measure academic skills—not just functional skills—for special populations. Improved understanding of patterns of language acquisition and the relationship between language skills and academic proficiency have supported the development of better tools for assessing English-language learners across many domains.

Increased Availability of Assessment Data The premise of NCLB is that if states and districts had more data to document their students' mastery of educational objectives, they would use that information to improve curricula and instructional planning. States and districts have indeed demonstrated a growing sophistication in the analysis and use of data. Improved technology has made it easier for educators and policy makers to have access to data and to use them, and more people are using them. However, the capacity to draw sound inferences from the copious data to which most policy makers and educators now have access depends on their training. As discussed below, this capacity has in many cases lagged behind the technology for collecting data.

Improved Reporting The combination of stricter reporting requirements under NCLB and improved technology has led states and districts to pay more attention to their reporting systems since 2002. Some have made marked improvements in presenting data in ways that are easy for users to understand and use to make effective decisions.[5]

Weaknesses

Greater Reliance on Multiple-Choice Tests In comparison with the assessments of the 1990s, today's state assessments are less likely to measure complex learning. Multiple-choice and short constructed-response items that are machine scorable predominate. Though valuable, these item types assess only a limited portion of the knowledge and skills that are called for in current standards.

More Focus on Tested Content Than on Standards Particularly in low-performing schools, test-based accountability has focused attention on standards, especially the subset of academic standards and content domain that is covered by the tests. Although this focus has had some positive effects, it has also had negative ones. States and districts have narrowed their curricula, placing the highest priority on tested subjects and on the content in those subjects that is covered on tests. The result has been emphasis on lower-level knowledge and skills and very thin alignment with the standards: for example, Porter, Polikoff, and Smithson (2009) found very low to moderate alignment between state assessments and standards—meaning that large proportions of content standards are not covered on the assessments (see also Fuller et al., 2006; Ho, 2008).

---

[5]Marion cited the Colorado Department of Education's website as a good example of innovative data reporting (see http://www.schoolview.org/ [accessed January 2010]).

More Narrow Test Preparation Because of the considerable pressure to make sure students meet minimum requirements on state assessments, many observers have noted an increased focus on so-called "bubble kids," those who are scoring just below cutoff points. A focus on drilling these students to get them above the passing level may often come at the expense of other kinds of instruction that may be more valuable in the long run. Discussants suggested that this focus on test preparation is particularly prevalent in schools serving poor and traditionally low-performing students; and the emerging result is a dual curriculum, in which already underserved children are not benefiting from the rigorous curriculum that is the ostensible goal of accountability (see, e.g., McMurrer, 2007). This approach often results in less attention to the needs of both high- and low-performing students.

Insufficient Rigor Many researchers and analysts regard current state assessments as insufficiently rigorous. Analysis of their cognitive demand suggests that they tend to focus on the lower levels of cognitive demands as defined in state standards and that they are less difficult than, for example, NAEP (see, e.g., Ho, 2008; Cronin et al., 2009). In general, the multiple-choice and short-answer items on which many state tests rely heavily are most frequently used to assess the recall of factual knowledge (rather than to assess students' abilities to synthesize or analyze knowledge, for example), and basic skills (rather than more complex thinking skills).

Challenges

Many of the challenges that presenters and discussants identified as most pressing mirrored the strengths and weaknesses. They identified opportunities not only to address the weaknesses, but also to build on many of the strengths in the current system.

Purposes of Testing For Goertz, any plans for improving assessment and accountability systems should begin with clear thinking about several questions: "What do we want to test and for what purpose? What kinds of information do we want to generate and for whom? What is the role of a state test in a comprehensive assessment system? What supports will educators need?" Assessments, Goetz said, whatever their nature, communicate goals to students and teachers. They signal what is valued, in terms of the content of curriculum and instruction and in terms of types of learning. Everyone in the system listens to the signal that testing sends, and they respond accordingly. Goertz suggested that current approaches may be coherent, in a sense, but many assessments are sending the wrong signals to students and teachers, because insufficient attention has been given to varying purposes for which they are actually being used.

The System as a Whole If tests are bearing too much weight in the current system, several participants said it is logical to ask whether every element of an accountability system must be represented by a test score. Measures of students' opportunity to learn and student engagement, as well as descriptive measures of the quality of the teaching and learning, may provide a valuable counterbalance to the influence of multiple-choice testing. It is important to balance the need for external accountability against other important goals for education.

Thus, in different ways, Marion, Goertz, and Herman each suggested that it is important to evaluate the validity of the entire system, seeking evidence that each element of the system serves its intended purpose. The goal for an accountability system should be to provide appropriate evidence for all intended users and to ensure that those users have the capacity and resources to use the information. The key question, Herman said, is clear: "Can we engineer the process well enough that we minimize the negative and maximize the positive consequences?" Clearly, she stressed, it does not make sense to rely on an annual assessment to provide all the right data for every user—or to measure the breadth and depth of the standards.

Looking at the system as a whole will entail not only consideration of intended and unintended consequences of assessments, but also a clear focus on the capacity of each element of the system to function as intended. However, Goertz pointed out, a more innovative assessment system—one that measures the most important instructional goals—cannot by itself bring about the changes that are desired. Support for the types of curriculum and instruction that foster learning, as well as such critical elements as teacher quality, is also needed.

Staff Capacity Many workshop participants spoke about the importance of developing a "culture of data use." Even as much more data has become available, insufficient attention has been paid to developing teachers' and administrators' capacity to interpret it accurately and use it to support their decision making. Ideally, a user-friendly information management system will focus teachers' attention on the content of assessment results so they can easily make correct inferences (e.g., diagnose student errors) and connect the evidence to specific instructional approaches and strategies. Teachers would have both the time to reteach content and skills students have not mastered and the knowledge of effective strategies to target the gaps.

System Capacity Looking more broadly at the capacity issue, Marion noted again that here has been a "three- or four-fold increase in the number of tests that are given without any corresponding increase in assessment personnel." Yet performance or other kinds of innovative assessments require more person-hours at most stages of the process than do multiple-choice assessments. These issues were discussed in the next session of the workshop, described in Chapter 2.

Reporting of Results Although there have been improvements in reporting, it has generally received the least attention of any aspect of the assessment system. NCLB has specific reporting requirements, and many jurisdictions have better data systems and better technology as a result. Nevertheless, even the best reports are still constrained by the quality of the data and the capacity of the users to turn these data into information, decisions, and actions.

2

Improving Assessments— Questions and Possibilities

There is no shortage of ideas about how states might improve their assessment and accountability systems. The shared goal for any such change is to improve instruction and student learning, and there are numerous possible points of attack. But, as discussed in Chapter 1, many observers argue that it is important to consider the system as a whole in order to develop a coherent, integrated approach to assessment and accountability. Although any one change—higher quality assessments, better developed standards, or more focused curricula—might have benefits, it would not lead to the desired improvement on its own. Nevertheless, it is worth looking closely at possibilities for each of the two primary elements of an accountability system: standards and assessments.

STANDARDS FOR BETTER INSTRUCTION AND LEARNING: AN EXAMPLE

Much is expected of education standards as a critical system component because they define both broad goals and specific expectations for students. They are intended to guide classroom instruction, the development of curricula and supporting materials, assessments, and professional development. Yet evaluations of many sets of standards have found them wanting, and they have rarely had the effects that were hoped and expected for them (National Research Council, 2008).

Shawn Stevens used the example of science to describe the most important attributes of excellent standards. She began by enumerating the most prevalent criticisms of existing national, state, and local science standards: that they include too much material, do not establish clear priorities among the material included, and provide insufficient interpretation of how the ideas included should be applied. Efforts to reform science education have been driven by standards—and have yielded improvements in achievement—but existing standards do not generally provide a guide for the development of coherent curricula. They do not support students in developing an integrated understanding of key scientific ideas, she said, which has been identified as a key reason that U.S. students do not perform as well as many of their international peers (Schmidt, Wang, and McKnight, 2005). Stevens described a model she and two colleagues developed that is based on current understanding of science learning, as well as a proposed process for developing such standards and using them to develop assessments (Krajcik, Stevens, and Shin, 2009).

Stevens and her colleagues began with the recommendations in a National Research Council (2005) report on designing science assessment systems: standards need to describe performance expectations and proficiency levels in the context of a clear conceptual framework and be built on sound models of student learning. Standards should be clear, detailed, and complete; reasonable in scope; and both rigorous and scientifically accurate. She briefly summarized the findings from research on learning in science that are particularly relevant to the development of such standards.

Integrated understanding of science is built on a relatively small number of foundational ideas that are central across the scientific disciplines—referred to as "big ideas"—such as the principle that the natural world is composed of a number of interrelated systems (see also National Research Council, 1996, 2005; Stevens, Sutherland, and Krajcik, 2009). These kinds of ideas allow both scientists and students to explain many sorts of observations and to identify connections among facts, concepts, models, and principles (National Research Council, 2005; Smith et al., 2006). Understanding of the big ideas helps learners develop detailed conceptual frameworks that, in turn, make it possible to undertake scientific tasks, such as solving problems, making predictions, observing patterns, and organizing and structuring new information. Learning complex ideas takes time and often happens as students work on tasks that force them to synthesize new observations with what they already knew. Students draw on a foundation of existing understanding and experiences as they gradually assemble bodies of factual knowledge and organize it according to their growing conceptual understanding.

The most important implication of these findings for standards is that they must be elaborated so that educators can connect them with instruction, instructional materials, and assessments, Stevens explained. That is, not only should a standard describe the subject matter it is critical for students to know, it should also describe how students should be able to use and apply that knowledge. For example, standards should not only describe the big ideas in declarative sentences, but also elaborate on the underlying concepts that are critical to developing a solid understanding of each big idea. Moreover, these concepts and ideas should be revisited throughout K-12 schooling so that knowledge and reasoning become progressively more refined and elaborated. Standards need to reflect these stages of learning. And because prior knowledge is so important to developing understanding, it is important that standards are specific about the knowledge students will need at particular stages to support each new level of understanding. Stevens also noted that standards need to address common misunderstandings and difficulties students have learning particular content so that instruction can explicitly target them; research has documented some of these. The approach of Stevens and her colleagues to designing rigorous science standards is based on previous work in the design of curricula and assessments, which they call construct-centered design (McTighe and Wiggins, 1998; Mislevy and Riconscente, 2005; Krajcik, McNeill, and Reiser, 2008; Shin, Stevens, and Krajcik, in press). The name reflects the goal of making the ideas and skills (constructs) that students are expected to learn, and that teachers and researchers want to measure, the focus for aligning curriculum, instruction, and assessment. Stevens described the six elements in the construct-centered design process that function in an interactive, iterative way, so that information gained from any element can be used to clarify or modify the product of another.

The first step is to *identify the construct*. The construct might be a concept (evolution or plate tectonics), a theme (e.g., size and scale or consistency and change), or a scientific practice (learning about the natural world in a scientific way). Stevens used the example of forces and interactions on the molecular and nano scales—that is, the idea that all interactions can be described by multiple types of forces, but that the relative impact of each type of force changes with scale—to illustrate the process.

The second step is to *articulate the construct, on the basis of expert knowledge of the discipline and related learning research*. This, Stevens explained, means explicitly identifying the concepts that are critical for developing understanding of a particular construct and defining the successive targets for students would reach in the course of their schooling, as they progress toward full understanding of the construct. This step is important for guiding the instruction at various levels.

Box 2-1 shows an example of the articulation of one critical concept that is important to understanding the sample construct (regarding forces and interactions on the molecular and nano scale). This articulation, which describes the upper level of K-12 understanding, is drawn from research on this topic; such research has not been conducted for many areas of science knowledge.

The articulation of the standard for this construct would also address the kinds of misconceptions students are likely to bring to this topic, which are also drawn from research on learning of this subject matter. For example, students

BOX 2-1
Articulation of the Idea That Electrical Forces Govern Interactions Between Atoms and Molecules

- Electrical forces depend on charge. There are two types of charge—positive and negative. Opposite charges attract; like charges repel.
- The outer shell of electrons is important in inter-atomic interactions. The electron configuration in the outermost shell/orbital can be predicted from the Periodic Table.
- Properties, such as polarizability, electron affinity, and electronegativity, affect how a certain type of atom or molecule will interact with another atom or molecule. These properties can be predicted from the Periodic Table.
- Electrical forces generally dominate interactions on the nano-, molecular, and atomic scales.
- The structure of matter depends on electrical attractions and repulsions between atoms and molecules.
- An ion is created when an atom (or group of atoms) has a net surplus or deficit of electrons.
- Certain atoms (or groups of atoms) have a greater tendency to be ionized than others.
- A continuum of electrical forces governs the interactions between atoms, molecules, and nanoscale objects.
- The attractions and repulsions between atoms and molecules can be due to charges of integer value, or partial charges. The partial charges may be due to permanent or momentary dipoles.
- When a molecule has a permanent electric dipole moment, it is a polar molecule.
- Instantaneous induced-dipole moments occur when the focus of the distribution shifts momentarily, thus creating a partial charge. Induced-dipole interactions result from the attraction between the instantaneous electric dipole moments of neighboring atoms or molecules.
- Induced-dipole interactions occur between *all* types of atoms and molecules, but increase in strength with an increasing number of electrons.
- Polarizability is a measure of the potential distortion of the electron distribution. Polarizable atoms and ions exhibit a propensity toward undergoing distortions in their electron distribution.
- In order to predict and explain the interaction between two entities, the environment must also be considered.

SOURCE: Krajcik, Stevens, and Shin (2009, p. 11).

might believe that hydrogen bonds occur between two hydrogen atoms or not understand the forces responsible for holding particles together in the liquid or solid state (Stevens, Sutherland, and Kajcik, 2009). This sort of information can help teachers make decisions about when and how to introduce and present particular material and help curriculum designers plan instructional sequences.

The third step is to *specify the way students will be expected to use the understanding that has been identified and articulated.* Stevens and her colleagues call this step developing "claims" about the construct. Claims identify the reasoning or cognitive actions students would do to demonstrate their understanding of the construct. (For this step, too, developers would need to rely on research on learning for the particular subject.) Students might be expected to be able to provide examples of particular phenomena, explain patterns in data, or develop and test hypotheses. For example, a claim related to the example in Box 2-1 might be: "Students should be able to explain the attraction between two objects in terms of the generation of opposite charges caused by an imbalance of electrons."

The fourth step is to *specify what sorts of evidence will constitute proof that students have gained the knowledge and skills described.* A claim might be used at more than one level because understanding is expected to develop sequentially across grades, Stevens stressed. Thus, it is the specification of the evidence that makes clear the degree and depth of students' understanding that are expected at each level. Table 2-1 shows the claim regarding opposite charges in the context of the cognitive activity and critical idea under which it nests, as well the evidence of understanding of this claim that might be expected of senior high school students. The evidence appropriate for say, middle school students, would be less sophisticated.

The fifth step is to *specify the learning and assessment tasks that students need to demonstrate, based on the elaborated description of the knowledge and skills students need.* The "task" column in Table 2-1 shows examples.

The sixth step is to *review and revise all the products to ensure that they are well aligned with one another.* Such a review might include internal quality checks conducted by the standards developers, as well as feedback from teachers or from content or assessment experts. Stevens said that pilot tests and field trials provide essential information, and review is critical to success.

Stevens and her colleagues were also asked to examine the draft versions of the common core standards for 12th grade English and mathematics that were developed by the Council of Chief State School Officers and the National Governors Association to assess how closely they conform to the construct-centered design approach. Their analysis noted that both sets of standards do describe how the knowledge they call for would be used by students, but that the English standards do not describe what sorts of evidence would be necessary to prove that a student had met the standards. The mathematics standards appeared to provide more elaboration.

TABLE 2-1 Putting a Claim About Student Learning in Context

Critical Idea	Cognitive Activity	Claim	Evidence	Task
Intermolecular Forces	Construct an explanation.	Students will be able to explain attraction between two objects in terms of the production of opposite charges caused by an imbalance of electrons.	Student work product will include – Students explain the production of charge by noting that only electrons move from one object to another object. – Students note that neutral matter normally contains the same number of electrons and protons. – Students note that electrons are negative charge carriers and that the destination object of the electrons will become negative, as it will have more electrons than protons. – Students recognize that protons are positive charge carriers and that the removal of electrons causes the remaining material to have an imbalance in positive charge. – Students cite the opposite charges of the two surfaces as producing an attractive force that hold the two objects together.	*Learning Task:* Students are asked to predict how pieces of tape will be attracted or repulsed by each other. *Assessment Task:* Students are asked to explain why the rubbing of fur against a balloon causes the fur to stick to the balloon.

SOURCE: Krajcik, Stevens, and Shin (2009, p. 14).

ASSESSMENTS FOR BETTER INSTRUCTION AND LEARNING: AN EXAMPLE

Assessments, as many have observed, are the vehicle for implementing standards, and, as such, have been blamed for virtually every shortcoming in education. There may be no such thing as an assessment task to which no one will object, Mark Wilson said, but it is possible to define what makes an assessment task good—or rather how it can lead to better instruction and learning. He provided an overview of current thinking about innovative assessment and described one example of an effort to apply that thinking, in the BEAR (Berkeley Evaluation and Assessment Research) System (Wilson, 2005).

An assessment task may affect instruction and learning in three ways, Wilson said. First, the inclusion of particular content or skills signifies to teachers, parents, and policy makers what should be taught. Second, the content or structure of an item conveys information about the sort of learning that is valued in the system the test represents. "Do we want [kids] to know how to select from four options? Do we want them to know how they can develop a project and work on it over several weeks and come up with an interesting result and present it in a proper format? These are the sorts of things we learn from the contents of the item," Wilson explained. And, third, the results for an item, together with the information from other items in a test, provide information that can spur particular actions.

These three kinds of influences often align with three different perspectives—(1) policy makers perhaps most interested in signaling what is most important in the curriculum, (2) teachers and content experts most interested in the messages about implications for learning and instruction, and (3) assessment experts most interested in the data generated. All three perspectives need to be considered in a discussion of what makes an assessment "good."

For Wilson, the most important characteristic of a good assessment system is coherence. A coherent system is one in which each element (of both summative and formative assessments) measures consistent constructs and contributes distinct but related information that educators can use. Annual, systemwide, summative tests receive the most attention, he pointed out, but the great majority of assessments that students deal with are those that teachers use to measure daily, weekly, and monthly progress. Therefore, classroom assessments are the key to effective instruction and learning, he emphasized. Building classroom assessments is more challenging than building large-scale summative ones—yet most resources go to the latter.

In some sense, Wilson pointed out, most state assessment systems are coherent. But he describes the current situation for many of them as "threat coherence," in which "large-scale summative assessment is used as a driving and constraining force, strait-jacketing classroom instructions and curriculum." He maintained that in many cases the quality of the tests and the decisions about what they should cover are not seen as particularly important—what matters is that they provide robust data and clear guidance for teachers. This sort of situation presents teachers with a dilemma: the classroom tests they use may either parallel the large-scale assessment or be irrelevant for accountability purposes. Thus, they can either focus on the tested material despite possible misgivings about what they are neglecting, or they can view preparing for the state test and teaching as two separate endeavors.

More broadly, Wilson said, systems that are driven by large-scale assessments risk overlooking important aspects of the curricula that cannot be adequately assessed using multiple-choice tests (just as some content cannot be easily assessed using projects or portfolios). Moreover, if the results of one systemwide assessment are used as the sole or principal indicator of performance on a set of standards that may describe a hundred or more constructs, it is very unlikely that student achievement on any one standard can be assessed in a way that is useful for educational planning. Results from such tests would support a very general conclusion about how students are doing in science, for example, but not more specific conclusions about how much they have learned in particular content areas, such as plate tectonics, or how well they have developed particular skills, such as making predictions and testing hypotheses.

Another way in which systems might be coherent is through common items, Wilson noted. For example, items used in a large-scale assessment might be used for practice in the classroom, or slightly altered versions of the test items might be used in interim assessments, to monitor students' likely performance on the annual assessment. The difficulty he sees with this approach to system coherence is that a focus on what it takes to succeed with specific items may distract teachers and students from the actual intent behind content standards.

When the conceptual basis—the model of student learning—underlying all assessments (whether formative or summative) is consistent, then the system is coherent in a more valuable way. It is even possible to go a step beyond this sort of system coherence, to what Wilson called "information coherence." In such a system, one would make sure not only that assessments are all developed from the same model of student learning, but also that they are explicitly linked in other ways. For example, a standardized task could be administered to students in many schools and jurisdictions, but delivered in the classroom. The task would be designed to provide both immediate formative information that teachers can use and consistent information about how well students meet a particular standard. Teachers would be trained in a process that ensured a degree of standardization in both test administration and evaluation of the results, and statistical controls could be used to monitor and verify the results. Similarly, classroom work samples based on standardized assignments could be centrally scored. The advantage of this approach is that it derives maximum advantage from each activity. The assessment task generates information and is also an important instructional activity; the nature of the assessment also com-

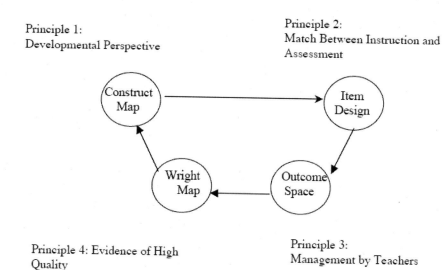

FIGURE 2-1 The BEAR System.
SOURCE: Wilson (2009, slide #20).

municates very directly with teachers about what sorts of learning and instruction are valued by the system (see Wilson, 2004).[1]

The BEAR System (Wilson, 2005) is an example of an assessment system that is designed to have information coherence. It is based on four principles, each of which has a corresponding "building block," see Figure 2-1. These elements function in a cycle, so that information gained from each phase of the process can be used to improve other elements. Wilson noted that current accountability systems rarely allow for this sort of continuous feedback and refinement, but that it is critical (as in any engineering system) to respond to results and developments that could not be anticipated.

The construct map defines what is to be assessed, and Wilson described it as a visual metaphor for the ways that students' understanding develops and, correspondingly, how their responses to items might change. Table 2-2 is an example of a construct map for an aspect of statistics, the capacity to consider certain statistics (such as a mean or a variance) as a measure of the qualities of a sample distribution.

---

[1]Another approach to using assessments conducted throughout the school year to provide accountability data is the Cognitively-Based Assessment of, for and as Learning (CBAL), a program currently under development at the Educational Testing Service (for more information, see http://eric.ed.gov/PDFS/ED507810.pdf [accessed August 2010].

TABLE 2-2 Sample Construct Map: Conception of Statistics

Conception of Statistics (CoS3): Objective	Student Tasks Specific to CoS3	Student/Teacher Response
	CoS3(f) Choose statistics by considering qualities of a particular sample.	– "It is better to calculate median because this data set has an extreme outlier. The outlier increases the mean a lot."
	CoS3(e) Attribute magnitude or location of a statistic to processes generating the sample.	– A student attributes a reduction in median deviation to a change in the tool used to measure an attribute.
	CoS3(d) Investigate the qualities of a statistic.	– "Nick's spreadness method is good because it increases when a data set is more spread-out."
	CoS3(c) Generalize the use of a statistic beyond its original context of application or invention.	– Students summarize different data sets by applying invented measures. – Students use average deviation from the median to explore the spreadness of the data.
CoS3. Consider statistics as measure of qualities of a sample distribution.	CoS3(b) Invent a sharable measurement process to quantify a quality of the sample.	– "In order to find the best guess, I count from the lowest to the highest and from the highest to the lowest at the same time. If I have an odd total number of data, the point where the two counting methods meet will be my best guess. If I have an even total number, the average of the two last numbers of my two counting methods will be the best guess."
	CoS3(a) Invent an idiosyncratic measurement process to quantify a quality of the sample based on tacit knowledge that the other may not share.	– "In order to find the best guess, I first looked at which number has more than others and I got 152 and 158 both repeated twice. I picked 158 because it looks more reasonable to me."

SOURCE: Wilson (2009, slide #23).

The item design specifies how students will be stimulated to respond and is the means by which the match between curriculum and assessment is established. Wilson described it as a set of principles that allow one to observe students under a set of standard conditions. Most critical is that the design specifications make it possible to observe each of the levels and sublevels described in the construct map. Box 2-2 shows a sample item that assesses one of the statistical concepts in the construct map in Table 2-2.

BOX 2-2
Sample Item Assessing Conceptions of Statistics

Kayla's Project

Kayla completes **four projects** for her social studies class. Each is worth **20 points.**

Kayla's Projects	Points Earned
Project 1	16 points
Project 2	18 points
Project 3	15 points
Project 4	???

The mean score Kayla received for **all four** projects was **17**.

Use this information to find the **number of points** Kayla received on **Project 4**. Show your work.

SOURCE: Wilson (2009, slide #25).

The "outcome space" on the lower right portion of Figure 2-1 is a general guide to the way students' responses to items developed in relation to a particular construct map will be valued. The more specific guidance developed for a particular item is used as the actual scoring guide, Wilson explained, which is designed to ensure that all of the information elicited by the task is easy for teachers to interpret. Figure 2-2 is the scoring guide for the "Kayla" item, with sample student work to illustrate the levels of performance.

The final element of the process is to collect the data and link it back to the goals for the assessment and the construct maps. The system relies on a multidimensional way of organizing statistical evidence of the quality of the assessment, such as its reliability, validity, and fairness. Item response models show students' performance on particular elements of the construct map across time and also allow for comparison within a cohort of students or across cohorts.

Wilson closed by noting that a goal for almost any large-scale test is to provide information that teachers can use in the classroom, but that this goal requires that large-scale and classroom assessments are constructed to provide information in a coherent way. He acknowledged, however, that implementing a system such as BEAR is not a small challenge. Doing so requires a deep analysis of the relationship between student learning, the curriculum, and instructional practices—a level of analysis not generally undertaken as part of test develop-

Kayla's Project Exemplar: Conceptions of Statistics (CoS)		
Levels	**Response Exemplars**	**Example of Student Response**
CoS3 D	Predict how a statistic is affected by changes in its components or otherwise demonstrate knowledge of relations among its components	"The differences between the mean and each score are -3, 1, -2, so the last difference must be 2 and the score must be 19."
CoS2 A	Calculate statistics indicating central tendency correctly. Guess and check strategies are acceptable.	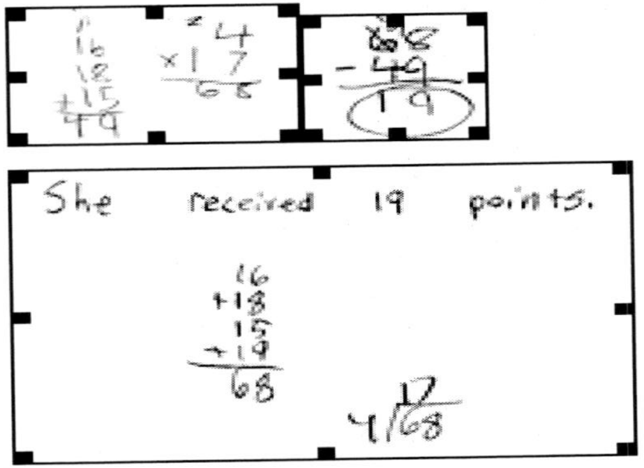

FIGURE 2-2 Scoring guide for sample item.
SOURCE: Wilson (2009, slide #27).

ment. Doing so also requires a readiness to revise both curricula and standards in response to the empirical evidence that assessments provide.

INNOVATIONS AND TECHNICAL CHALLENGES

Stephen Lazer reflected on the technical and economic challenges of pursuing innovative assessments on a large scale from the point of view of test developers. He began with a summary of current goals for improving assessments:

- increase use of performance tasks to measure a growing array of skills and obtain a more nuanced picture of students;
- rely much less on multiple-choice formats because of limits on what they can measure and their perceived impact on instruction;
- use technology to measure content and skills not easily measured using paper-and-pencil formats and to tailor assessments to individuals; and
- incorporate assessment tasks that are authentic—that is, that ask students to do tasks that might be done outside of testing and are worthwhile learning activities in themselves.

If this is the agenda for improving assessments, he pointed out, "it must be 1990." He acknowledged that this was a slight overstatement: progress has been made since 1990, and many of these ideas were not applied to K-12 testing until well after 1990. Nevertheless, many of the same goals were the focus of reform two decades ago, and an honest review of what has and has not worked well during 20 years of work on innovative assessments can help increase the likelihood of success in the future.

A review of these lessons should begin with clarity about what, exactly, an innovative assessment is, he said. For some, Lazer suggested, it might be any item format other than multiple choice, yet many constructed-response items are not particularly innovative because they only elicit factual recall. Some assessments incorporate tasks with innovative presentation features, but they may not actually measure new sorts of constructs or produce richer information about what students know and can do. Some computer-based assessments fall into this category. Because they are colorful and interesting, some argue that they are more engaging to students, but they may not differ in more substantive ways from the assessments they are replacing. If students click on a choice, rather than filling in a bubble, "we turn the computer into an expensive page-turner," he pointed out. Moreover, there is no evidence that engaging assessments are more valid or useful than traditional ones, and the flashiness may disguise the wasting of a valuable opportunity.

What makes an assessment innovative, Lazer argued, is that it expands measurement beyond the constructs that can be measured easily with multiple-choice items. Both open-ended and performance-based assessments offer possibilities for doing this, as does technology. Performance assessments offer a number of possibilities: the opportunity to assess in a way that is more directly relevant to the real-world application of the skills in question, the opportunity to obtain more relevant instructional feedback, a broadening of what can be measured, and the opportunity to better integrate assessment and instruction.

Use of Computers and Technology Computers make it possible to present students with a task that could not otherwise be done—for example, by allowing students to demonstrate geography skills using an online atlas when distributing printed atlases would have been prohibitively expensive. Equally important, though, is that students will increasingly be expected to master technological skills, particularly in science, and those kinds of skills can only be assessed using technology. Even basic skills, such as writing, for which most students now use computers almost exclusively whether at home or at school, may need to be assessed by computer to ensure valid results. Computer-based testing and electronic scoring also make it possible to tailor the difficulty of individual items to a test taker's level and skills. Furthermore, electronic scoring can provide results quickly and may make it easier to derive and connect formative and summative information from items.

Cost Perhaps the most significant challenge to using these sorts of innovative approaches is cost, Lazer said. Items of this sort can be time consuming and expensive to develop, particularly when there are few established procedures for this work. Although some items can be scored by machine, many require human scoring, which is significantly more expensive and also adds to the time required to report results. Automated scoring of open-ended items holds promise for reducing the expense and turnaround time, Lazer suggested, but this technology is still being developed. The use of computers may also have hidden costs. For example, very few state systems have enough computers in classrooms to test large numbers of students simultaneously. When students cannot be tested simultaneously, the testing window must be longer, and security concerns may mean that it is necessary to have wide pools of items and an extended reporting window. Many of these issues need further research.

Test Development Test developers know how to produce multiple-choice items with fairly consistent performance characteristics on a large scale, and there is a knowledge base to support some kinds of constructed-response items. But for other item types, Lazer pointed out, "there is really very little in the way of operational knowledge or templates for development." For example, simulations have been cited as a promising example of innovative assessment, and there are many interesting examples, but most have been designed as learning experiments, not assessments. Thus, in Lazer's view, the development of ongoing assessments using simulations is in its infancy. Standard techniques for analyzing the way items perform statistically do not work as well for many constructed-response items as for multiple-choice ones—and not at all for some kinds of performance tasks. For many emerging item types, there is as yet no clear model for getting the maximum information out of them, so some complex items might yield little data.

The Role of a Theoretical Model The need goes deeper than operational skills and procedures, however, Lazer said. Multiple-choice assessments allow test developers to collect data that support inferences about specific correlations—for example, between exposure to a particular curriculum and the capacity to answer a certain percentage of a fairly large number of items correctly—without requiring the support of a strong theoretical model. For other kinds of assessments, particularly performance assessments that may include a much smaller number of items or observations, a much stronger cognitive model of the construct being measured is needed. Without such a model, Lazer noted, one can write open-ended or computer-based items that are not very high in quality, something he suggested happened too frequently in the early days of performance assessment. Moreover, even a well-developed model is no guarantee of the quality of the items. The key challenge is not to mistake authenticity for validity. Validity depends on the claim one wants to make, it is very important that the construct be defined accurately and that the item truly measures the skills and knowledge it is intended to measure.

It can also be much more difficult to generalize from assessments that rely on a relatively small number of tasks. Each individual task may measure a broader construct than do items on conventional tests, but at the cost of yielding a weaker measure of the total domain, of which the construct is one element. And since the items are likely to be more time consuming for students, they will complete fewer of them. There is likely to be a fairly strong person-task interaction, particularly if the task is heavily contextualized.

It is also important to be clear about precisely what sorts of claims the data can support. For example, it may not be possible to draw broad conclusions about scientific inquiry skills from students' performance in a laboratory simulation related to a pond ecosystem. With complex tasks, such as simulations, there may also be high interdependence among the observations that are collected, which also undermines the reliability of each one. These are not reasons to avoid this kind of item, Lazer said, but he cautioned that it is important to be aware that if generalizability is low enough, the validity of the assessment is jeopardized. Assessing students periodically over a time span, or restricting item length, are possible ways of minimizing these disadvantages, but each of these options presents other potential costs or disadvantages.

Scoring Lazer underlined that human scoring introduces another source of possible variation and limits the possibility of providing rapid results. In general, the complexity of scoring for some innovative assessments is an important factor to consider in a high-stakes, "adequate yearly progress environment," in which high confidence in reliability and interrater reliability are very important. A certain degree of control over statistical quality is important not only for comparisons among students, but also for monitoring trends. Value-added modeling and other procedures for examining a student's growth over time and the effects of various inputs, such as teacher quality, also depend on a degree of statistical precision that can be difficult to achieve with some emerging item types.

Equating Lazer noted that a related issue is equating, which is normally accomplished through the reuse of a subset of a test's items. Many performance items cannot be reused because they are memorable. And even when they can be reused, it can be difficult to ensure that they are scored in exactly the same way across administrations. Although it might be possible to equate by using other items in a test, if they are of a different type (e.g., multiple choice), the two parts may actually measure quite different constructs, so the equating could actually yield erroneous results. For similar reasons, it can be very difficult to field test these items, and though this is a mundane aspect of testing, it is very important for maintaining the quality of the information collected.

Challenges for Students Items that make use of complex technology can pose a challenge to students taking the tests, Lazer said. It may take time for students to learn to use the interface and perform the activities the test requires, and the complexity may affect the results in undesired ways. For example, some students may score higher because they have greater experience and facility with the technology, even if their skill with the construct being tested is not better than that of other students.

Conflicting Goals For Lazer, the key concern with innovative assessment is the need to balance possibly conflicting goals. He repeated what others have noted—that the list of goals for new approaches is long: assessments should be shorter and cheaper and provide results quickly; they should include performance assessment; they should be adaptive; and they should support teacher and principal evaluation. For him, this list highlights that some of the challenges are "know-how" ones—that can presumably be surmounted with additional effort and resources. Others are facts of life. Psychometricians may be working from outdated cognitive models, and this can be corrected. But it is unlikely that further research and development will make it possible to overcome the constraints imposed when both reliability and validity, for example, are important to the results.

"This doesn't mean we should give up and keep doing what we're doing,"

Lazer concluded. These are not insurmountable conflicts, but each presents a tradeoff. He said the biggest challenge is acknowledging the choices. To develop an optimal system will require careful thinking about the ramifications of each feature. Above all, Lazer suggested, "we need to be conscious of the limits of what any single test can do." He enthusiastically endorsed the systems approaches described earlier, in which different assessment components are designed to meet different needs, but in a coherent way.

LOOKING FORWARD

A few themes emerged in the general discussion. One was that the time and energy required for the innovative approaches described—specifying the domain, elaborating the standards, validating that model of learning—is formidable. Taking this path would seem to require a combination of time, energy, and expertise that is not typically devoted to test development. However, the BEAR example seems to marry the expertise of content learning, assessment design, and measurement in a way that offers the potential to be implemented in a relatively efficient way. The discussion of technical challenges illustrated the many good reasons that the current testing enterprise seems to be stuck in what test developers already know how to do well.

This situation raised two major questions for workshop participants. First: Is the $350 million total spending planned for the Race to the Top Initiative enough? Several participants expressed the view that assessment is an integral aspect of education, whether done well or poorly, but that its value could be multiplied exponentially if resources were committed to develop a coherent system. Second: What personnel should be involved in the development of new assessment systems? The innovation that is required may be more than can be expected from test publishers. A participant joked that the way forward might lie in putting cognitive psychologists and psychometricians in a locked room until they resolved their differences—the challenge of balancing the competing imperatives each group raises is not trivial.

A final word from another participant, that "it's the accountability, stupid," reinforced a number of other comments. That is, the need to reduce student achievement to a single number derives from the punitive nature of the current accountability system. It is this pressure that is responsible for many of the constraints on the nature of assessments. Changing that context might make it easier to view assessments in a new light and pursue more creative forms and uses.

3

Recent Innovative Assessments

Since the early 1990s, there have been many small-scale experiments to implement assessments that were in some sense innovative. Some have not been sustainable—for a range of reasons—but others are ongoing. What made these programs innovative? What can be learned from them? Brian Stecher and Laura Hamilton provided an overview of both current innovations and those that have not continued, and a panel of people connected with the programs offered their comments.

Stecher pointed out that the sort of test that is currently typical—multiple choice, paper and pencil—was innovative when it was introduced on a large scale in the early 20th century, but is now precisely the sort that innovators want to replace. So, in that sense, an innovative assessment could be defined simply as one that is not a multiple-choice, paper-and-pencil test. That is, a test might be innovative because it:

- incorporates prompts that are more complex than is typical in a printed test, such as hands-on materials, video, or multiple types of materials;
- offers different kinds of response options—such as written responses, collections of materials (portfolios), or interactions with a computer— and therefore requires more sophisticated scoring procedures; or
- is delivered in an innovative way, usually by computer.

These aspects of the structure of assessments, Stecher suggested, represent a variety of possibilities that are important to evaluate carefully. Several other themes worth exploring across programs, he noted, such as the challenges related to technical quality (e.g., reliability, fairness, and validity), were discussed in a previous workshop session (see Chapter 2). Tests with innovative characteristics (like any tests) send signals to educators, students, and parents about the learning that is most valued in the system—and in many cases innovative testing has led to changes in practice. Testing also has costs, including a burden in both time and resources, which are likely to be different for different innovative assessments. Testing also provokes reactions from stakeholders, particularly politicians.

LOOKING BACK

Performance and other kinds of alternative assessments were popular in the 1990s, when 24 states were using, developing, or exploring possibilities for using one of these approaches (Stecher and Hamilton, 2009). Today, those kinds of alternative assessments are much less prevalent. States have moved away from these approaches, primarily for political and budget reasons, but a look at several of the most prominent examples highlights some lessons, Brian Stecher explained. Individuals who had experience with several of the programs added their perspectives.

Vermont

Vermont was a pioneer in innovative assessment, having implemented a portfolio-based program in writing and mathematics in 1991 (Stecher and Hamilton, 2009). The program was designed both to provide achievement data that would permit comparison of schools and districts and to encourage instructional improvements. Teachers and students in grades 4 and 8 collected work to represent specific accomplishments, and these portfolios were complemented by a paper-and-pencil test.

Early evaluations raised concerns about scoring reliability and the validity of the portfolio as an indicator of school quality (Koretz et al., 1996). After efforts to standardize scoring rubrics and selection criteria, the reliability improved, but evaluators concluded that the scores were not accurate enough to support judgments about school quality.

The research (Koretz et al., 1996) showed that teachers did alter their practice in response to the assessment: for example, they focused more on problem solving in mathematics. Many schools began using portfolios in other subjects, as well, because they found them useful. However, some critics said that teachers did not uniformly demonstrate a clear understanding of the intended criteria for selecting student work, and others commented that teachers began overemphasizing the specific strategies that were included in the standardized rubrics. Costs were high—$13 per student just for scoring. The program was discontinued in the late 1990s, primarily because of concerns about the quality of the scores.

Kentucky

The Kentucky Instructional Results Information System (KIRIS) was closely watched because it was part of a broad-based response to a state supreme court ruling that the education system was unconstitutional (Stecher and Hamilton, 2009). The assessment as a whole covered reading, writing, social science, science, mathematics, arts and humanities, and practical living/vocational studies. The state made significant changes to its schools and accountability system, and it implemented performance assessment in 1992. The program was designed to support school-level accountability; other indicators, such as dropout, attendance, and teacher retention rates, were also part of the accountability system.

Brian Gong described the assessment program, which tested students in grades 4, 8, and 12 using some traditional multiple-choice and short-answer tests, but relying heavily on constructed-response items (none shorter than half a page). KIRIS used matrix sampling to provide school accountability information. Many performance assessments asked students to work both in groups and individually to solve problems and to use manipulatives in hands-on tasks. KIRIS included locally scored portfolios in writing and mathematics.

Evaluations of KIRIS showed that teachers changed their practice in desirable ways, such as focusing greater attention on problem solving, and they generally attributed the changes they made to the influence of open-ended items and the portfolios (Koretz et al., 1996). Despite the increased burden in time and resources, teachers and principals supported the program.

As with the Vermont program, however, evaluators found problems with both reliability and validity. The portfolios were assigned a single score (in the Vermont program there were scores for individual elements), and teachers tended to assign higher scores than the independent raters. In addition, teachers reported that they believed score gains were more attributable to familiarity with the program and test preparation than to general improvement in knowledge and skills, and research supported this belief, finding that teachers tended to emphasize the subjects tested in the grades they taught, at the expense of other subjects. Further support for this finding came from scores on the National Assessment of Educational Progress (NAEP) and the American College Testing Program (now called the ACT) for Kentucky students: they did not show growth comparable to that shown on KIRIS (Koretz and Barron, 1998). KIRIS was replaced with a more traditional assessment after only 6 years, in 1998—though that assessment also included constructed-response items—and the state continued to use portfolios to assess writing until 2009.

Maryland

The Maryland School Performance Assessment Program (MSPAP), implemented in 1991, assessed reading, writing, language usage, mathematics, science, and social science at grades 3, 5, and 8 (Stecher and Hamilton, 2009). The program was designed to measure school performance and to influence instruction; it used matrix sampling to cover a broad domain and so could not provide individual scores. The entire assessment was performance based, scored by teams of Maryland teachers.

MSPAP did not have any discrete items, Steve Ferrara noted. All the items were contained within tasks organized around themes in the standards; many integrated more than one school subject, and many required group collaboration. The tasks included both short-answer items and complex, multipart response formats. MSPAP included hands-on activities, such as science experiments, and asked students to use calculators, which was controversial at the time.

Technical reviews indicated that the program met reasonable standards for both reliability and validity, although the group projects and a few other elements posed challenges. Evaluations and teacher reports also indicated that MSPAP had a positive influence on instruction. However, some critics questioned the value of the scores for evaluating schools, noting wide score fluctuations. Others objected to the "Maryland learning outcomes" assessed by the MSPAP. The MSPAP was replaced in 2002 by a more traditional assessment that provides individual student scores, a requirement of the No Child Left Behind (NCLB) Act.

Washington

The Washington Assessment of Student Learning (WASL), implemented in 1996, assessed learning goals defined by the state legislature: reading; writing; communication; mathematics; social, physical, and life sciences; civics and history; geography; arts; and health and fitness (Stecher and Hamilton, 2009). The assessment used multiple-choice, short-answer, essay, and problem-solving tasks and was supplemented by classroom-based assessments in other subjects. WASL produced individual scores and was used to evaluate schools and districts; it was also expected to have a positive influence on instruction.

Evaluations of WASL found that it met accepted standards for technical quality. The evaluations also found some indications that teachers adapted their practice in positive ways, but controversy over its effects affected its implementation. For example, the decision to use WASL as a high school exit exam was questioned because of low pass rates, and fluctuating scores raised questions about its quality. The WASL was replaced during the 2009-2010 school year with an assessment that uses multiple-choice and short-answer items. However, the state has retained some of the classroom-based assessments.

A workshop participant with experience in Washington, Joe Willhoft, pointed out several factors that affected the program's history.[1] First was that the program imposed a large testing burden on teachers and schools. After NCLB was passed, the state was administering eight tests in both elementary and middle schools, with many performance assessment features that were complex and time consuming. Many people were not expecting the testing to consume so much time. This initial reaction to the program was compounded when early score gains were followed by much slower progress. The result was frustration for both teachers and administrators.

This frustration, in turn, fueled a growing concern in the business community that state personnel were not managing the program well. Willhoft said that the initial test development contract was very inexpensive, considering the nature of the task, but when the contract was rebid costs escalated dramatically. And then, as public opinion was turning increasingly negative about the program, the policy makers who had initially sponsored it and worked to build consensus in its favor were leaving office, because of the state's term limit law, so there were few political supporters to defend the program when it was challenged. This program was also replaced with a more traditional one.

California

The California Learning Assessment System (CLAS), which was implemented in 1993, assessed reading, writing, and mathematics, using performance techniques such as group activities, essays, and portfolios (Stecher and Hamilton, 2009). Some items asked students to reflect on the thinking that led to their answers. Public opposition to the test arose almost immediately, as parents complained that the test was too subjective and even that it invaded students' privacy by asking about their feelings. Differences of opinion about CLAS led to public debate about larger differences regarding the role assessment should play in the state. Questions also arose about sampling procedures and the objectivity of the scoring. The program was discontinued after only 1 year (Kirst and Mazzeo, 1996).

NAEP Higher-Order Thinking Skills Assessment Pilot

An early, pioneering effort to explore possibilities for testing different sorts of skills than were generally being targeted in standardized tests was conducted by NAEP in 1985 and 1986 (Stecher and Hamilton, 2009). NAEP staff developed approximately 30 tasks that used a variety of formats (paper and pencil, hands-on, computer administered, etc.) to assess such

---

[1]Willhoft is currently Assistant Superintendent for Assessment and Student Information in the state of Washington.

higher-order mathematics and science skills as classifying, observing and making inferences, formulating hypotheses, interpreting data, designing an experiment, and conducting a complete experiment. NAEP researchers were pleased with the results in many respects, finding that many of the tasks were successful and that conducting hands-on assessments was both feasible and worthwhile. But the pilots were expensive and took a lot of time, and school administrators found them demanding. These item types were not adopted for the NAEP science assessment after the pilot test.

Lessons from the Past

For Stecher, these examples make clear that the boldest innovations did not survive implementation on a large scale, and he suggested that hindsight reveals several clear explanations. First, he suggested, many of the programs were implemented too quickly. Had developers and policy makers moved more slowly and spent longer on pilot testing and refining, it might have been possible to iron out many of problems with scoring, reporting, reliability, and other complex elements of the assessments. Moreover, he noted that many of the states pushed forward with bold changes without necessarily having a firm scientific foundation for what they wanted to do. At the same time, the costs and the burdens on students and schools were high, which made it difficult to sustain support and resources when questions arose about technical quality. People questioned whether the innovations were worth the cost and effort.

Another factor, Stecher said, is that many states did not adequately take into account the political and other concerns that would affect public approval of the innovative approaches. In retrospect, it seemed that many of the supporters of innovative testing programs had not adequately educated policy makers and the public about the goals for the programs and how they would work. One reason for this lack, however, is that states were not always able to reconcile differences among policy makers and assessment developers regarding the role the assessment was to play. When there was a lack of clarity or agreement about goals, it was difficult to sustain support for the programs when problems arose. A final consideration for many states was the need to comply with NCLB requirements.

CURRENT INNOVATIONS

Even though many of the early programs did not survive intact, innovative assessment approaches remain in wide use. Laura Hamilton reviewed current examples of three of the most popular innovations: performance assessment, portfolios, and technology-supported assessment.

Performance Assessment

Essays are widely used in K-12 assessments today, particularly in tests of writing and to supplement multiple-choice items in other subjects (Stecher and Hamilton, 2009). Essays have been incorporated in the SAT (formerly known as the Scholastic Aptitude Test) and other admissions tests and are common in NAEP. They are also common in licensure and certification tests, such as bar examinations.

The K-12 sector is not currently making much use of other kinds of performance assessment, but other sectors in the United States are, as are a number of programs in other countries. One U.S. example is the Collegiate Learning Assessment (CLA), which measures student learning in colleges and universities, is administered on-line, and uses both writing tasks and performance tasks in response to a wide variety of stimuli.

The assessment system in Queensland, Australia, is designed to provide both diagnostic information about individual students and results that can be compared across states and territories. It includes both multiple-choice items and centrally developed performance tasks that can be used at the discretion of local educators and are linked to the curriculum. At the secondary level, the assessment incorporates not only essays, but also oral recitations and other performances. Performance tasks are scored locally, which raises concerns about comparability, but school comparisons are not part of the system, so the pressure is not as heavy on that issue as in the United States. Indeed, Hamilton noted, many aspects of Queensland's system seem to have been developed specifically to avoid problems in the U.S. system, such as score inflation and narrowed curricula.

Other programs use hands-on approaches to assess complex domains. For example, the U.S. Medical Licensing Examination (USMLE) has a clinical skills component in which prospective physicians interact with patients who are trained participants. The trained patient presents a standardized set of symptoms so that candidates' capacity to collect information, perform physical examinations, and communicate their findings to patients and colleagues can be assessed. Hamilton noted that this examination may be the closest of any to offering an assessment that approximates the real-life context for the behavior the assessment is designed to predict—a key goal for performance assessment. Nevertheless, the program has encountered technical challenges, such as limited variability among tasks (the standardized patients constitute the tasks), interrater reliability, and the length of time required (8 hours to complete the assessment).

These examples, Hamilton suggested, indicate the potential for performance assessment, but also the challenges in terms of cost, feasibility, and technical quality. For example, sampling remains a difficult problem in performance assessment. Multiple tasks are generally needed to support inferences about a particular construct, but including them all poses a significant burden on the program.

Another difficulty is the tension between the goal of producing scores that support comparisons across schools or jurisdictions and the goal of using the assessment process itself to benefit teachers and students. The Queensland program and the essay portion of the bar exams administered by states both involve local educators or other local officials in task selection and scoring, and this may limit the comparability of scores. When the stakes attached to the results are high, centralized task selection and scoring may be preferred, but at the cost of not involving teachers and affecting instruction. Hamilton also noted that none of the program examples operate with a constraint like that of the NCLB, which requires that multiple consecutive grades be tested every year. Indeed, she suggested, "it would be difficult to adopt any of these approaches in today's K-12 testing system without making significant changes to state policy surrounding accountability."

Portfolios

Portfolio-based assessments have much less presence in K-12 testing than they once had, but they are used in other sectors in the United States and in a number of other nations. In the United States, the National Board for Professional Teaching Standards (NBPTS), which identifies accomplished teachers (from among candidates who have been teaching for a minimum of several years), asks candidates to assemble a portfolio of videotaped lessons that represent their teaching skills in particular areas. This portfolio supplements other information, collected through computer-based assessments, and allows evaluators to assess a variety of teaching skills, including so-called soft skills, practices, and attitudes, such as the capacity to reflect on a lesson and learn from experience. The assessment is extremely time-consuming, requiring up to 400 hours of a candidate's time over 12-18 months. Because of the relatively low number of tasks, the program has relatively low reliability numbers, and it has also raised concerns about rater variability. However, it has received high marks for validity because it is seen as capturing important elements of teaching.

Technology-Supported Assessment

Computers have long been widely used in assessment, Hamilton explained, although for only a fairly limited range of purposes. For the most part they have been used to make the administration and scoring of traditional multiple-choice and essay testing easier and less expensive. However, recent technological developments have made more innovative applications more feasible, and they have the potential to alter the nature of assessment.

The increasing availability of computers in schools will make it easier to administer computerized-adaptive tests in which items are presented to a candidate on the basis of his or her responses to previous items. Many states had turned their attention away from this technology because NCLB requirements seemed to preclude its use in annual grade-level testing. However, revisions to NCLB appear likely to permit, and perhaps even encourage, the use of adaptive tests, which is already common in licensure and certification contexts.

The use of computerized simulations to allow candidates to interact with people or objects that mirror the world is another promising innovation. This technology allows students to engage in a much wider range of activities than is traditionally possible in an assessment situation, such as performing an experiment that requires the lapse of time (e.g., plant growth). It can also allow administrators to avoid many of the logistical problems of providing materials or equipment by simulating whatever is needed. Such assessments can provide rapid feedback and make it possible to track students' problem-solving steps and errors. Medical educators have been pioneers in this area, using it as part of the USMLE: the examinee is given a patient scenario and asked to respond by ordering tests or treatments and then asked to react to the patient's (immediate) response. Minnesota has also used simulations in its K-12 assessments (see Chapter 4).

Automated essay scoring is also beginning to gain acceptance, despite skepticism from the public. Researchers have found high correlations between human scores and automated scores, and both NAEP and the USMLE are considering using this technology. Moreover, the most common current practice is for computer-based scoring to be combined with human-based scoring. This approach takes advantage of the savings in time and resources and also provides a check on the computer-generated scores. However, some problems remain. Automated scoring systems have been developed with various methodologies, but the software generally evaluates human-scored essays and identifies a set of criteria and weights that can predict the human-assigned scores. The resulting criteria are not the same as those a human would use: for example, essay length, which correlates with other desirable essay traits, would not itself be valued by a human scorer. In addition, the criteria may not have the same results when applied across different groups of students: that is, test developers need to ensure that differences between human rater scores and scores assigned by computers do not systematically favor some subgroups of students over others. Some observers also worry that the constraints of automated scoring might limit the kinds of prompts or tasks that can be used.

In Hamilton's view, technology clearly offers significant potential to improve large-scale assessment. It opens up possibilities for assessing new kinds of constructs and for providing detailed data. It also offers possibilities for more easily assessing students with disabilities and English language learners, and it can provide an effective means of integrating classroom-based and large-scale assessment.

A few issues are relevant across these technologies, Hamilton noted. If students bring different levels of skill with computers to a testing situation, as is likely, the differences may affect their results: this outcome is supported by some research. Schools are increasingly likely to have the necessary infrastructure to administer such tests, but this capacity is still unequally distributed. Teachers trained to prepare students for these sorts of assessments and accurately interpret the results are also not equally distributed among schools. Another issue is that the implications of computer-based approaches for validity and reliability have not been thoroughly evaluated.

4

Political Experiences and Considerations

A recurring theme at both workshops was tradeoffs. Many of the discussions highlighted that political considerations are a very important aspect of almost all decisions about assessment and accountability, and that they have played a critical role in the history of states' efforts with innovative assessments. Veterans of three programs—the Maryland School Performance Assessment Program (MSPAP), the Kentucky Instructional Results Information System (KIRIS), and the Minnesota Comprehensive Assessment in Science—reflected on the political challenges of implementing these programs and the factors that have affected the outcomes for each.

MARYLAND

MSPAP was a logical next step for a state that had been pursuing education reform since the 1970s, Steve Ferrara explained. Maryland was among the first to use school- and system-level data for accountability, and the state also developed the essay-based Maryland Writing Test in the 1980s. That test, one of the first to use human scoring, set the stage for MSPAP. MSPAP was controversial at first, particularly after the first administration yielded pass rates as low as 50 percent for 9th graders. However, the test had a significant influence on writing instruction and scores quickly rose.

The foundation for MSPAP was a Commission on School Performance established in 1987 by then governor William Schaeffer, which outlined ambitious goals for public education and recommended the establishment of content standards that would focus on higher order thinking skills. The commission also explicitly recommended that the state adopt an assessment that would not rely solely on multiple-choice items and that could provide annual report cards for schools.

Ferrera said that the governor's leadership was critical in marshalling the support of business and political leaders in the state. Because the Maryland governor appoints members of the state board of education, who, in turn, appoint the superintendent of public instruction, the result was "a team working together on education reform." This team was responding to shifting expectations for education nationally, as well as a sense that state and district policy makers and the public were demanding assurances of the benefits of their investment in education. Ferrara recalled that the initial implementation went fairly smoothly, owing in part to concerted efforts by the state superintendent and others to communicate clearly with the districts about the goals for the program and how it would work and to solicit their input.

Most school districts were enthusiastic supporters, but several challenges complicated the implementation. The standards focused on broad themes and conceptual understanding, and it was not easy for test developers to design tasks that would target those domains in a way that was feasible and reliable. The way the domains were described in the standards led to complaints that the assessment did not do enough to assess students' factual knowledge. The schedule was also exceedingly rapid, with only 11 months between initial planning and the first administration. The assessment burden was great—for example, 9 hours over 5 days for 3rd graders. There were also major logistical challenges posed by the manipulatives needed for the large number of hands-on items.

The manipulatives not only presented logistical challenges, they also revealed a bigger challenge for teachers. For example, teachers who had not even been teaching science were asked to lead students through an assessment that included experiments. Teachers were also being asked more generally to change their instruction. The program involved teachers in every phase—task development, scoring, etc.—and Ferrara said that the teachers' involvement was one of the most important ingredients in its early success.

As discussed in an earlier workshop session (see Chapter 3), there is evidence that teachers changed their practice in response to MSPAP (Koretz et al., 1996; Lane et al., 1999). Nevertheless, many people in the state began to oppose the program. Criticisms of the content and concern about the lack of individual student scores were the most prominent complaints, and the passage of the No Child Left Behind (NCLB) Act in 2002 made the latter concern urgent. The test was discontinued in that year.

For Ferrara, several key lessons can be learned from the history of MSPAP:

- Involving stakeholders in every phase of the process was very valuable; doing so both improved the quality of the program and built political acceptance.

- It paid to be ambitious technically, but it is not necessary to do everything at once. For example, an assessment program could have a significant influence on instruction without being exclusively composed of open-ended items. If one makes a big investment in revolutionary science assessment, there will be fewer resources and less political capital for other content areas.
- It was short-sighted to invest the bulk of funds and energy in test development at the expense of ongoing professional development.

KENTUCKY

Brian Gong explained that the 1989 Kentucky Supreme Court decision that led to the development of KIRIS was intended to address both stark inequities in the state's public education system and the state's chronic performance at or near the bottom among the 50 states. The resulting Kentucky Education Reform Act (KERA) was passed in 1990, with broad bipartisan and public support. It was one of the first state education reform bills and included innovative features, such as a substantial tax increase to fund reform; a restructuring of education governance; the allocation of 10 paid professional development days per year for teachers; and a revamped standards, assessment, and accountability system.

KERA established accountability goals for schools and students (proficiency within 20 years) and called for an assessment system that would be standards based, would rely primarily on performance-based items, and would be contextualized in the same way high-quality classroom instruction is. The result, KIRIS, met these specifications, but the developers faced many challenges. Most critically, the court decision had actually identified the outcomes to be measured by the assessment. Those outcomes were the basis for the development of academic expectations and then core content for assessment, but the definitions of the constructs remained somewhat elusive. Educators complained that they were not sure what they were supposed to be doing in the classroom, Gong said, and in the end it was the assessment that defined the content that was valued, the degree of mastery that was expected, and the way students would demonstrate that mastery. But developing tasks to assess the standards in valid ways was difficult, and the assessment alone could not provide sufficient information to influence instruction.

There were other challenges and adaptations, Gong noted. It was difficult to collect data for standard setting using the complex, multifaceted evidence of students' skills and knowledge that KIRIS was designed to elicit. Equating the results from year to year was also difficult: most of the tasks were very memorable and could not be repeated. Alternate strategies—such as equating KIRIS to assessments in other states, judgmental equating, and equating to multiple-choice items—presented both psychometric challenges and practical disadvantages. KIRIS also initially struggled to maintain standards of accuracy and reliability in scoring the constructed-response items and portfolios, and adaptations and improvements were made in response to problems.

Guidelines for the development of portfolios had to be strengthened in response to concerns about whether they truly reflected students' work. With experience, test developers also gradually moved from holistic scoring of portfolios to analytic scoring in order to obtain more usable information from the results. The state also faced logistical challenges, for example, with field testing and providing results in time for accountability requirements.

Nontechnical challenges emerged as well. The state was compelled to significantly reduce its assessment staff and to rely increasingly on consultants. School accountability quickly became unpopular, Gong explained, and many people began to complain that the aspirations were too high and to question the assertion that all students could learn to high levels. Philosophical objections to the learning outcomes assessed by KIRIS also emerged, with some people arguing that many of them intruded on parents' prerogatives and invaded students' privacy. The so-called math and reading "wars"—over the relative emphasis that should be given to basic skills and fluency as opposed to broader cognitive objectives—fueled opposition to KIRIS. Finally, there were changes in the state's political leadership that decreased support for the program, and it did not survive an increasingly contentious political debate; KIRIS was ended in 1998.

For Gong there are several key lessons from the Kentucky experience:

- Clear definitions of the constructs to be measured and the purposes and uses of the assessment are essential. No assessment can compensate for poorly defined learning targets.
- The design of the assessment should be done in tandem with the design of the intended uses of the data, such as accountability, so that they can be both coherent and efficient.
- The people who are proposing technical evaluations and those who will be the subject of them should work together in advance to consider both intended and unintended consequences, particularly in a politically charged context.
- Anyone now considering innovative assessments for large-scale use should have a much clearer idea of how to meet technical and operational challenges than did the pioneering developers of KIRIS in the 1990s.
- Current psychometric models, which support traditional forms of testing, are inconsistent with new views of both content and cognition and should be applied only sparingly to innovative assessments. The field should invest in the development of improved models and criteria (see, e.g., Shepard, 1993; Mislevy, 1998).

MINNESOTA

Dirk Mattson explained that Minnesota's Comprehensive Assessment Series II (MCA-II) was developed in response to NCLB, so the state was able to benefit from the experiences of states that had already initiated innovative assessments. Some existing assessments in some subjects could be adapted, but the MCA-II in science, implemented in 2008, presented an opportunity to do something new. State assessment staff were given unusual latitude to experiment, Mattson said, because science had not been included in the NCLB accountability requirements.[1]

The result is a scenario-based assessment delivered on computers. Students are presented with realistic representations of classroom experiments, as well as phenomena that can be observed. Items—which may be multiple choice, short or long constructed response, or figural (i.e., students interact with graphics in some way)—and are embedded in the scenario. This structure provides students with an opportunity to engage in science at a higher cognitive level than would be possible with stand-alone items.

Mattson emphasized that the design of the science assessment grew out of the extensive involvement of teachers from the earliest stages. Teachers rejected the idea of an exclusively multiple-choice test, but a statewide performance assessment was also not considered because a previous effort had ended in political controversy. The obvious solution was a computer-delivered assessment, despite concerns about the availability of the necessary technology in schools. The developers had the luxury of a relatively generous schedule: conceptual design began in 2005, and the first operational assessment was given in 2008. This schedule allowed time for some pilot testing at the district level before field testing began in 2007.

A few complications have arisen. First, Minnesota statute requires regular revision of education standards, so the science standards were actually being revised before the prior ones had been assessed, but assessment revision was built into the process. Second, in 2009 the state legislature, facing severe budget constraints, voted to make the expenditure of state funds on human scoring of assessments illegal.[2] More recently, the state has contemplated signing on to the "common core" standards and is monitoring other changes that may become necessary as a result of the Race to the Top initiative or reauthorization of the federal Elementary and Secondary Education Act.

---

[1] The technical manual and other information about the program are available at http://education.state.mn.us/MDE/Accountability_Programs/Assessment_and_Testing/Assessments/MCA/TechReports/index.html [accessed April 2010].

[2] State money could still be used for machine scoring of assessments. Because Minnesota has no board of education, the legislature is responsible for overseeing the operations of the department of education; federal dollars were used to support human scoring.

In reflecting on the process so far, Mattson noted that despite the examples of other innovative assessment programs, many MCA elements were new and had to be developed from scratch. These elements included operations, such as means of conveying what was needed to testing contractors, estimating costs, and supporting research and development efforts. The new elements also included parts of the fundamental design, and Mattson noted that often the content specialists were far ahead of the software designers in conceptualizing what could be done. Technical challenges—from designing a test security protocol to preparing schools to load approximately 300-475 megabytes of test content onto their servers—required both flexibility and patience. A Statewide Assessment Technology Work Group helped identify and address many of the technical challenges, and Mattson pointed to this group as a key support.

For Mattson, it is important that the developers were not deterred by the fact that there were no paths to follow in much of development process. The success of the assessment thus far, in his view, has hinged on the fact that the state was able to think ambitiously. The leaders had enthusiastic support from teachers, as well as grant funding and other community support, which allowed them to sustain their focus on the primary goal of developing an assessment that would target the skills and knowledge educators believed were most important. The flexibility that has also been a feature of the MCA since the beginning—the state assessment staff's commitment to working with and learning from all of the constituencies concerned with the results—should allow them to successfully adapt to future challenges, Mattson said.

STRATEGIC IMPLICATIONS

The three state examples, suggested Lorraine McDonnell, highlight the familiar tension between the "missionaries" who play the important role of seeking ways to improve the status quo and those who raise the sometimes troublesome questions about whether a proposed solution addresses the right problem, whether the expected benefits will outweigh the costs, and whether the innovation can be feasibly implemented. She distilled several policy lessons from the presentations.

First, for an assessment to be successful, it is clear that the testing technology has to be well matched to the policy goals the assessment is intended to serve. Accurate educational measurement may be a technical challenge, but assessment policy cannot be clearly understood independent of its political function. Whether the function is to serve as a student- or school-level accountability device, to support comparisons across schools or jurisdictions, or to influence the content and mode of classroom instruction, what is most important is to ensure that the goals are explicitly articulated and agreed on. McDonnell observed that in many states test developers and politicians had not viewed the function of the state assessment in the same way. As a result, test developers could not meet the policy makers' expectations, and support for the assessment weakened. When policy makers expect the test to serve multiple purposes, the problem is most acute—and policy makers may not agree among themselves about the function of an assessment.

It is also very important that the testing system is integrated into the broader instructional system, McDonnell said. This idea was an element of the argument for systemic reform that was first proposed during the 1990s (Smith and O'Day, 1991) and has been prominent in reform rhetoric, but it has not played a major role in the current common standards movement. She pointed out that although the conditions that truly support effective teaching and learning should be central, they "appear once again to have been relegated to an afterthought." Support is needed to strengthen instructional programs, as well as assessment programs. Like many workshop participants, McDonnell highlighted the importance of a comprehensive and coherent system of standards, instruction, and assessment.

States and the federal government have tended, she suggested, to select instruments that were easy to deploy—such as tests—and to underinvest in such measures as curricula and professional development that could help to build schools' capability to improve education. Yet unless teachers are provided with substantial opportunities to learn about the deeper curricular implications of innovative assessments and to reshape their instruction in light of that knowledge, the result of any high-stakes assessment is likely to be more superficial test preparation, which McDonnell called "rubric-driven instruction." This conflict between policy pressure for ambitious improvements in achievement and the weak capability of schools and systems to respond was an enduring dilemma during the first wave of innovation, in the 1990s, and McDonnell suggested that it has not been resolved.

Yet another lesson, McDonnell said, is that policy makers and test designers need to understand the likely tradeoffs associated with different types of assessments and the need to decide which goals they want to advance and which ones they are willing to forgo or minimize. The most evident tension is between using tests as accountability measures and using them as a way to guide and improve instruction. As earlier workshop discussions showed, McDonnell said, these two goals are not necessarily mutually exclusive, but pursuing both with a single instrument is likely to make it difficult to obtain high-quality results.

This lesson relates to another, which may be obvious, McDonnell suggested, but appears to be easily overlooked: if a process is to be successful, every constituency that will be affected by an assessment must have ample opportunity to participate throughout its development. The differing perspectives of psychometricians and curriculum developers, for example, need to be reconciled if an assessment system is to be successful, but parents, teachers, and other interests need to be involved as well. If developers fail to fully understand and take into account public attitudes, they may encounter unexpected opposition to their plans. Conveying the rationale for an assessment approach to policy makers and the public, as well as the expected benefits and costs, may require careful planning and concerted effort.

It is often at the district level that the critical communications take place, and too often, McDonnell said, district leaders have not been involved in or prepared for this important aspect of the process. The benefit of clear and thorough communication is that stakeholders are more likely to continue to support a program through technical difficulties if they have a clear understanding of the overall goals.

Finally, McDonnell stressed, people need to remember that the implementation of innovative assessments takes time. It is very important to build in an adequate development cycle that allows for gradual implementation and for adaptation to potential problems. In several of the experiences discussed at the workshop, rushed implementation led to technical problems, undue stress on teachers and students, and a focus on testing formats at the expense of clear connections to curriculum. In several states, testing experts acquiesced to political pressure to move quickly in a direction that the testing technology could not sustain. Programs that have implemented innovative features gradually, without dismantling the existing system, have had more flexibility to adapt and learn from experience.

These policy lessons, as well as a growing base of technical advances, can be very valuable for today's "missionaries," McDonnell said. However, although past experience provides lessons, it may also have left a legacy of skepticism among those who had to deal with what were in some cases very disruptive experiences. Fiscal constraints are also likely to be a problem for some time to come, and it is not clear that states will be able to sustain new forms of assessment that may be more expensive than their predecessors after initial seed funding is exhausted. She also noted that the common standards movement and the Race to the Top Initiative have not yet become the focus of significant public attention, and there is no way to predict whether they will become the objects of ideological controversies, as have past education reforms. None of these are reasons not to experiment with new forms of assessment, McDonnell concluded, but "they are reasons for going about the enterprise in a technically more sophisticated way than was done in the past and to do it with greater political sensitivity and skill."

5

Coherent Assessment Systems

The workshop presentations and discussions highlighted the disadvantages of many current approaches to assessment and the desirability of a coherent system in which multiple approaches are used to collect formative and summative information about student learning to meet the needs of students, teachers, administrators, policy makers, and the public. As Diana Pullin noted, the approach mandated by the No Child Left Behind (NCLB) Act has demonstrated that assessments can generate data that people will attend to, but the result is not necessarily any marked improvement in teaching or learning. Federal and state officials have placed tremendous demands on assessments, during a period when funds to support their development have been shrinking. Tests have been stretched to cover too many purposes, with results that are widely viewed as unsatisfactory.

The question to ask now, Pullin observed, is how states might move from present practices to innovative learning-based assessments embedded in coherent systems that foster improved learning and more appropriate accountability. With that goal in mind, Joan Herman provided an examination of coherent assessment systems and the key features they should have to serve the dual purposes of supporting student learning and providing accountability. The second part of this chapter summarizes subsequent discussions in which policy makers, researchers, and practitioners shared their perspectives on the challenges of establishing a coherent assessment system.

CHARACTERISTICS OF A COHERENT SYSTEM

It is a propitious time for a move toward coherent assessment systems, Herman observed. The Race to the Top funding, the opportunity for states to sign on to the common core learning standards, and converging confidence in the potential of new kinds of assessments—particularly formative assessments—combine to produce an important window of opportunity. Fortunately, Herman said, there is a strong body of research on which to base new approaches.[1]

Herman delineated key elements of a coherent assessment system: that it is a system of assessments, not a single assessment; that it is coherent with specified learning goals; and that its components collectively support multiple uses in a valid manner.

On the value of a system, as opposed to a single assessment, Herman noted that most tests used for accountability purposes today target only a limited subset of the learning goals that school systems set for their students. "If we want to know whether kids can write," Herman observed, "we need something more than an editing test with multiple-choice questions. If we want to know whether kids can innovate, engage in inquiry, or collaborate with others, again, multiple-choice or short-answer tests are not giving the depth of information that we really need."

This is critically important not only because tests communicate what it is important for students to learn, as was emphasized throughout both workshops, but also because their results will only support sound decision making if they provide a rich picture of what students know and are able to do. Thus, by moving from an exclusive reliance on multiple-choice and short-answer items to systems that also include performance and other kinds of assessments, states can better serve accountability purposes: they will be able to answer questions about important capacities not well addressed by current tests, such as depth of thinking and reasoning, the ability to apply knowledge and solve problems, the ability to communicate and collaborate, and the ability to master new technology. At the same time, the kinds of measures that teachers need on a daily basis in their classrooms are quite different from the annual or through-course kinds of measures that policy makers use to monitor progress on a more macro level.

Assessment systems are able to provide that rich picture if they are coherent with established goals for learning. This is not a controversial idea, Herman observed, but she distinguished four types of coherence. The most fundamental type of coherence is that among models of how students learn, the design of assessments, and the interpretation of their results, as illustrated in Figure 5-1. In Herman's view, the fundamental coherence most states have now is orga-

---

[1]Herman mentioned three reports in particular (American Educational Research Association, American Psychological Association, and National Council on Measurement in Education, 1999; National Research Council, 2001, 2005), but noted that that there are many other resources.

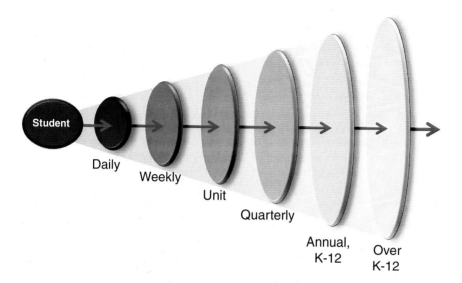

FIGURE 5-1 Developmental coherence learning goals.
SOURCE: From Joan Herman, Next Generation Assessment Systems: Toward Coherence and Utility. Used with permission from The National Center for Research on Evaluation, Standards, and Student Testing (CRESST) and by The Regents of the University of California supported under the Institute of Education Science (IES) U.S. Department of Education. Copyright © 2010.

nized around the material covered in annual statewide tests—not necessarily key learning goals.

The second kind of coherence, horizontal coherence, expands the alignment to assessment and instruction. This is generally assumed to be part of state accountability systems, Herman noted, but she questioned whether states really pose the question of whether students who have been taught the material identified in learning goals actually do better on annual statewide tests than students who have not. Third, developmental coherence describes instruction that builds student learning over time, progressing through daily, weekly, quarterly, and annual goals to deeper understanding. As Figure 5-1 illustrates, this sort of coherence extends across grades K-12, and tests ought to assess, in developmentally appropriates ways, the key competencies that students need to build along the way to college readiness.

The fourth kind of coherence is vertical coherence. The users of assessments at each level—the classroom, school, district, and state—have different information needs, but the means of producing that information can and should be aligned with learning goals. Thus, the design of very different types of assessments—from activities embedded in classroom instruction for the purpose of providing immediate information about short-term learning goals to annual instruments designed to provide broad information about the effectiveness of a curriculum or the status of student subgroups—needs to reflect fundamental coherence.

Herman provided a matrix of assessment purposes not unlike the one presented earlier in the workshop series (see Chapter 1), but designed to illustrate the ways in which varying purposes can be met by a system that incorporates a range of assessment instruments linked by shared learning goals: see Table 5-1.

In developing a complex system to meet these multiple purposes, Herman explained, it is important to stay focused on fundamental validity—to ask to what extent the system, both in its individual measures and collectively, serves its intended purposes. When a single assessment is used to serve all purposes, it ends up serving none very well. Thus, it is important to identify all of the consequences of an assessment. Validity is not simply a matter of psychometric quality, Herman pointed out, and she identified some of the most important criteria for different sorts of assessments that should be incorporated into analysis of the validity of systems: see Table 5-2.

Assessments can help support improvements in many aspects of education, but they are not sufficient in themselves to change practice: Herman echoed others' comments about the importance of coherence with other aspects of the system (teacher preparation and professional development, curriculum, etc.). She concluded with the acknowledgment that designing such a coherent system is an extremely complex challenge: "this is not just a matter of going into a room and figuring out what to do." Existing technology and methodologies will need to be expanded. "That will take time," she observed, "and there is no one right answer." In her view, the best path forward is to explore multiple alternatives.

PERSPECTIVES ON IMPLEMENTATION

Several discussants were asked to comment on what they viewed as the most important considerations for implementing a new approach to assessment and accountability.

The Policy Process

Roy Romer, a former school superintendent and governor of Colorado, focused on the process that states are going through to forge new approaches to assessment and on the challenge of communicating new goals and strategies to the people who will need to accept them if they are to be successful. First, he pointed out that the process that is unfolding—in which states are grouping themselves into consortia to apply for federal grants that will support the

TABLE 5-1 Assessment Purposes[*]

Assessment	Assessment Type	Primary Users	Use—Based on Race to the Top
Annual	On-demand annual	• State • District • Schools • Teachers • Parents • Students • Public	• Teacher/principal/school effectiveness • Professional development needs • School and district quality • General feedback, both curriculum and student strengths/weaknesses • Recognize and build on excellence • Status/growth toward college readiness
Through Course Exams	End-of-unit Mid-term Semester End-of-course	• Schools • Teachers • Students	• Assign grades • Inform short- and medium-term decisions about curriculum and instruction • Identify struggling students
School/ District	Benchmark	• Districts • Schools • Teachers • Students	• Inform short- and medium-term decisions about curriculum and instruction • Identify struggling students • Identify struggling teachers • Identify struggling schools • Identify promising practices • Identify year-to-year trends
Classroom	Formative Curriculum-embedded Student work Discourse Discussion	• Teachers • Students	• Inform immediate and short-term teaching and learning • Identify struggling students

[*]Created based on a review of the expectations in the Race to the Top Assessment Program (2010). See Comprehensive Assessment System grant, http://www2.ed.gov/programs/racetothetop-assessment/index.html [accessed September 2010].
SOURCE: From Joan Herman, Next Generation Assessment Systems: Toward Coherence and Utility. Used with permission from the National Center for Research on Evaluation, Standards, and Student Testing (CRESST) and by the Regents of the University of California supported under the Institute of Education Science, U.S. Department of Education. Copyright © 2010.

development of new kinds of assessment systems—is one that, by design, has no leader.

This approach has an advantage, in his view, because a key strategy for opposing a political change is to identify a figure to represent the change and then to associate that figure with negative images in order to marshal opposition to the change. With multiple states participating in three different consortia,

TABLE 5-2 Validity Criteria for Assessment Systems

Purpose	Criteria
Accountability Assessments	• Learning-based, aligned • Comprehensive • Fair, sensitive to growth on full continuum • Precise • Comparable • Transferable—predicts subsequent success • Sensitive to instruction • Educative, models good practice • Consequences are appropriate and those affected have capacity to use them and respond to results
Monitoring/Supervision Assessments	• Suitable for intended use • Predictive • Provide reliable diagnosis • Based on defined learning trajectories • Instructionally tractable* • Timely • Educative • Consequences are appropriate and those affected have capacity to use them and respond to results
Formative Assessments	• Learning-based • Continuous • Support learning/instructional value • Diagnostic • Instructionally tractable for teachers and students [see above] • Unique—responds to individual and class • Educative • Consequences are appropriate and those affected have capacity to use them and respond to results

*The phrase "instructionally tractable" is used to mean results that provide information that teachers can use in planning next steps in instruction, teaching and learning.
SOURCE: From Joan Herman, Next Generation Assessment Systems: Toward Coherence and Utility. Used with permission from The National Center for Research on Evaluation, Standards, and Student Testing (CRESST) and by The Regents of the University of California supported under the Institute of Education Science (IES) U.S. Department of Education. Copyright © 2010.

this sort of opposition will be difficult.[2] Yet this approach also means that the result will be whatever some group of entities can agree to.

Romer suggested that at some point that process might need some structure. For him, some issues to consider might include agreement on what will

---

[2]Since the workshop, three consortia have been formed and formally applied for Race to the Top assessment grants. There are two parts to the grant, with different requirements. Two of the consortia have applied for Part A and one has applied for Part B.

be shared among the states and what will not. In order for assessment to be comparable, there must be a significant common component, but states will need the flexibility to vary some portion for their own purposes. Should the ratio be 70 percent comparable and 30 percent flexible or something else? How ought it to be fixed? Will multiple contractors be involved in developing and administering components of a consortium's assessment system, and, if so, how will their work be coordinated? Will there be a single, shared digital platform for groups of states—or even for the nation?

Romer also outlined the characteristics he views as most important for new assessment systems. They need to be affordable over the long term. They need to be internationally benchmarked and also benchmarked within the states, which means that state tests must be substantially comparable to one another. Perhaps more challenging will be to convey to parents and the public why the tests that are given to students at each grade are critical—that at each level they set the standards for what students need to know and be able to do to stay on track for success in college and the workplace. Considering the fast pace at which technology and the global economy are changing, this is a critical responsibility for public education, but one that may not yet be fully appreciated. A key question to ask, then, is "is it too expensive to ask the right questions—the ones that really help make sure the student is prepared for the next step?" Romer used the example of flight training to illustrate why the critical job of testing is to show whether a student has really learned what he or she needs to know and be able to do: tests used to certify that pilots are ready to fly have to be able to identify those who are not ready, regardless of the cost because if they do not they are useless.

Romer also noted that it is both a creative and a challenging time for public education. Politics have "allowed us to talk nationally about standards and assessments, but not about curriculum," he pointed out. The risk in that is that states will focus so much on tests and standards that they will overlook curriculum, teacher training, and other key elements of an aligned system. Communicating effectively about this will be key to success, he stressed. In the current political climate, "people are deeply worried about the financial future of their families." They understand that education will be key to their children's futures. It is very important "to tell them the truth about the nation's educational health—and to identify a path" for progress.

Curriculum-Embedded Assessments

Assessment "of, as, and for learning" was the theme of Linda Darling-Hammond's presentation. She agreed with Romer that curriculum and assessment are intertwined, and that students "are not entering a multiple-choice world." Like many others at the two workshops, she emphasized that readiness for college and 21st century careers requires not just basic skills and factual knowledge of the sort most frequently covered on standardized tests, but also the ability to find, evaluate, synthesize, and use knowledge. In order to be able to learn in changing contexts and to frame and solve nonroutine problems, students and workers will need knowledge and skills that are transferable, as well as skills in thinking, problem solving, design, teamwork, and communication.

This conception of learning supported a significant change in the approach to assessment in Hong Kong, Darling-Hammond explained, and it was the context in which the phrase "assessment of, as, and for learning" was coined. She noted that education reform initiatives in many high-achieving countries have focused on higher-order thinking skills. More specifically, they have focused on assessing the kinds of performance they want students to develop. Many countries, she observed, do not use multiple-choice assessments at all, and those that do balance them with other measures that capture complex knowledge and skills. When assessment is developed to be "of and for learning," the tasks themselves both convey what students should be learning and provide an opportunity to examine students' understanding. In most high-achieving nations, she added, teachers are integrally involved in developing and scoring on-demand and curriculum-embedded performance measures, which are combined to yield a total score on the examination. These experiences give them the opportunity to engage closely with the standards and the assessments and to consider carefully what good quality work looks like.

She summarized the key elements of this approach to assessment:

1. an integrated system of curriculum and assessment provides tests that are worth "teaching to" because they focus on the content and skills addressed by high-quality instruction;
2. teachers' involvement in developing, scoring, and using the results of assessments, which improves their understanding of the curriculum and the standards and thus helps them improve their instruction; and
3. assessments that evaluate the most valuable kinds of student work and reasoning skills and thus provide valuable information to both teacher and students.

Changes in Hong Kong demonstrate the effectiveness of this approach, she explained. Their education ministry has begun to replace traditional examinations with school-based tasks delivered in a variety of ways. These include oral presentations, portfolios or samples of work often done to specific specifications, field work investigations, lab work design projects, and the like—many are both delivered and scored by computer. She argued that these tasks are more valid assessments because they include outcomes that cannot be readily assessed using a one-time examination format. Other countries have similar systems, though some stress the standardization of the task more than others. One example is the General Certificate of Secondary Education offered students ages 14-16 in

England, Wales, and Northern Ireland, which has a range of assessments embedded in the curriculum as well as an end-of-course examination component.[3] As part of the literacy assessment, for example, students are asked to produce responses to different kinds of texts, to do certain kinds of imaginative writing, speaking, and listening activities, and to do information writing. Another example is Singapore's A-level examinations, which also include a combination of externally set examinations, long-term projects conducted to particular specifications, and school-based practical assessments.[4] Among the tasks required for the science examination is to design and conduct a scientific investigation and prepare a lengthy research paper documenting the work.

Curriculum-embedded tasks, Darling-Hammond explained, can more easily address central concepts and modes of inquiry than stand-alone assessments can. They can also more easily provide both summative and formative information, and they can allow for more detailed investigation of skills and knowledge also assessed in other components of an assessment system, for other purposes. She suggested that the United States is well behind other countries in this regard, though she noted that Connecticut has included in its assessment a science task for 9th- and 10th-grade students. Although it is not used for high-stakes purposes, it is designed to measure inquiry skills using an extended task that is structured and standardized and conducted in the classroom over an extended period of time.[5] The end-of course exam then revisits some of the concepts addressed in the curriculum-based task.

Darling-Hammond closed with her recommendations to states considering new assessment approaches that include curriculum-based components. They should

- develop systems for auditing and guiding teacher-scored work;
- provide time and training for teachers and school leaders;
- use technology to support teachers' participation in scoring and their training, as well as assessment delivery; and
- evaluate costs and manage development to ensure that the assessment system is feasible and sustainable.

Computer-Based Testing

Tony Alpert described the Oregon Assessment of Knowledge and Skills (OAKS), which is a program that has stressed the involvement of teachers: they

---

[3]See http://www.direct.gov.uk/en/EducationAndLearning/QualificationsExplained/DG_10039024 [accessed June 2010].

[4]See http://www.seab.gov.sg/ [accessed June 2010].

[5]The state also uses curriculum-embedded tasks at other levels; see http://www.sde.ct.gov/sde/cwp/view.asp?a=2618&q=320890&sdenav_gid=1757 [accessed June 2010].

write all of the state's assessment items and also score all of the assessments of writing. The system is now delivered almost exclusively online, he explained, though it took the state about 5 years to reach that level. Students have up to three opportunities during the school year to take the assessments. They receive their results immediately, and within 15 minutes of testing, teachers have access to those results, as well as aggregate results at the classroom, school, district, and state level. Education service districts, entities that support school districts with many logistical challenges, provide technical support for online testing.

Oregon had several reasons for moving to computer-based testing, Alpert explained. First, education officials concluded that investing in computer infrastructure rather than disposable paper-based assessments and shipping would be a better use of resources. Districts were expected to save money, and even if there were no savings, investment would be focused on infrastructure with lasting value. Computer-based testing would also allow the state to provide adaptive testing and instant results and to provide certain kinds of accommodations (for special needs students) not possible with paper-based testing. It has been difficult to make comparisons between the online system and its paper-based predecessor, in part because current costs for the former system are not available. Nevertheless, human scoring has been reduced by 45 percent, and many of the costs are not related to quantity so they do not rise with the number of students or administrations.

Online delivery also allowed the state to implement adaptive testing that could provide summative information as well as formative information. Specifically, Alpert noted, such testing allows them to better support both high- and low-performing students and to better track all students' incremental progress. He suggested that students may be more highly motivated to perform well when the bulk of the items they see are at a difficulty level that matches their ability and when opportunities for cheating—as well as motivation for teachers to focus on unconstructive test preparation—are reduced.

Alpert noted that adaptive testing also improves test validity by making it possible to measure the entire breadth of content standards every year, since testing is not limited to what can be contained in a finite number of booklets. Field testing can be done more efficiently because students, rather than schools, are the unit of analysis. This feature reduces potential errors in linking, Alpert explained, and also makes it easier to detect problematic items. Tests could be adapted on a variety of dimensions, he added, not just student ability and content standards. Oregon plans to explore additional possibilities, such as adapting based on the standard error of the measure or on student motivation. Alpert noted that the standard error of measurement has been lower for the computer-based testing than for the state's paper-based testing: see Figure 5-2.

Oregon officials also saw important advantages to allowing students multiple opportunities to take the tests, Alpert explained. When students can demonstrate their progress over time and have multiple opportunities to learn from and act

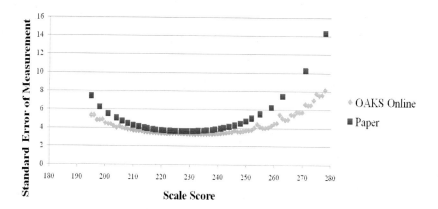

FIGURE 5-2 Standard error of measurement by scale score and assessment mode, grade 8 mathematics.
NOTE: OAKS = Oregon Assessment of Knowledge and Skills.
SOURCE: Alpert and Slater (2010, slide #7). Reprinted with permission from Dr. Tony Alpert and Dr. Stephen Slater of Oregon Department of Education.

on information about their progress, the officials reasoned, both they and their teachers would be more likely to use test results to improve achievement. The state officials also expected that the test results would support more valid interpretations because there would be less variance unrelated to the constructs being measured. Because the span of time within which testing can occur each year is long, the tests can more easily meet a variety of purposes and provide results when they are needed. Districts and schools can tailor testing schedules according to the availability of resources (e.g., computers, bandwidth) and can also integrate timelines for accountability reporting with the pace of instruction.

In Alpert's view, Oregon's assessment is well aligned to the breadth of the state's content standards (and thus horizontally coherent), but its heavy reliance on multiple-choice items means that there are limits to its capacity to measure them in depth. The system currently includes some performance assessment, but it does not count those tasks for federal accountability purposes. Teachers' involvement in writing and scoring assessment items, as well as professional development activities focused on the use of data to support student achievement, contribute to vertical coherence. Opportunities for multiple assessments of incremental progress contribute to developmental coherence. Still, the system does not yet fit the model of coherence described by Herman and others; he offered a roadmap for how it could move closer to that model: see Figure 5-3.

Fully implementing this model in Oregon would be a challenge, Alpert acknowledged, and would require

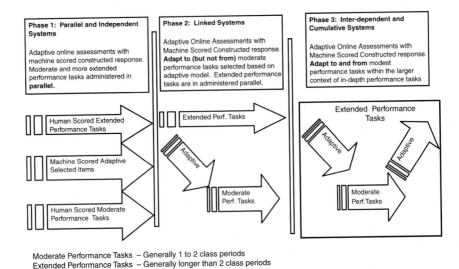

FIGURE 5-3 Roadmap for horizontal coherence of assessments with adaptive item selection.
SOURCE: Reprinted with permission from Dr. Tony Alpert and Dr. Stephen Slater of Oregon Department of Education.

- flexibility,
- professional development to support the use and interpretation of student data,
- item banks large enough to support assessment of a range of student abilities across the breadth of the content and cognitive complexity of a subject,
- robust software that can support efficient computer-based performance assessments,
- robust approach to measuring student performance, and
- adequate computers and supporting infrastructure.

BOARD EXAMINATION SYSTEMS

The goals and strategies characteristic of coherent systems are in many ways not new, Marc Tucker observed. Several centuries ago, Oxford and Cambridge Universities replaced their system of interviewing candidates for admission with a system in which they provided the schools from which most candidates came with clear descriptions of the preparation they would need and used an exam to confirm that the candidates were well prepared. Their goal, Tucker explained, was to develop exams that came as close as possible to eliciting the sorts of thinking and work production they would ask of matriculating students. When new universities were later founded, beginning in the 1830s, the standards became more formally established to ensure that all were holding students to the same standards.

These exams, in Tucker's view, were measuring the same sorts of higher-order thinking skills that are described today as 21st century skills. The schools that were preparing British students for university-level study were asked to teach them to think critically, to analyze and synthesize information from a wide variety of sources, and to produce useful products from their analysis, as well as to be able to both lead and cooperate to work collaboratively. "It is the whole list except learning how to twitter," he joked, and the only difference is that today the goal almost everywhere is to provide all students with these skills, not just those who are being groomed as future leaders.

In the United States, however, a very different testing tradition emerged from the work of psychiatrists and other pioneers of scientific psychological and educational measurement. U.S. public schools had extremely diverse curricula, and thus as the new principles of measurement began to be applied to education, the natural course was to develop tests that were curriculum neutral—the exact opposite of the approach that had developed in England. The new standardized tests that began to emerge in the 1940s and 1950s were inexpensive and efficient, Tucker explained, but they did not benefit from the British perspective. "You will never find out whether students can write a 10-page history research paper . . . by administering a computer-scored multiple-choice test . . . [nor from such a test could you determine] whether they can read two newspaper articles on the same subject; compare them and figure out what is fact, what is fiction; analyze the differences; and come up with a considered view of their own," he said.

This is critical, in Tucker's view, because the United States is behind other countries: it is "burdened with an approach to testing which is very well suited to testing basic skills and very ill adapted to testing the skills that are most important." Tweaks to the existing approach will not be sufficient, he argued, despite the fact that much in it is very valuable. He advocates that the United States look closely at the board examination systems used in many of the highest-performing countries in the world, and he cited studies from the Programme for International Student Assessment (PISA) that indicate that those systems are among the most important factors that explain those countries' success (Bishop, 1997; Fuchs and Woessman, 2007). Among the countries that use this approach are Australia, Belgium, Canada, England, Hong Kong,[6] the Netherlands, New Zealand, and Singapore.

In general, board examinations are used at the secondary level and are based on a core curriculum that is set for students through the age of 16 or so.

---

[6]Hong Kong is an administrative region of the People's Republic of China.

A syllabus for each course and instructional materials are provided to guide teachers, and the exam, usually a set of essays, is closely based on the syllabus. The syllabus specifies the level of skill expected, as well the material to be read and covered. The composite exam score generally also includes scores for work done in class during the year and scored by the teacher. Teacher training directly linked to the curriculum and course syllabi is a critical element.

Tucker stressed that all of these elements together would not be as effective as they are without the requirement that students pass a set of examinations in order to qualify for the next stage of study or work. Because students are focused not on logging 4 years in secondary school, but rather on what they need to accomplish to reach particular goals, he argued, they are highly motivated and clear about why they are studying particular material.

A number of these kinds of programs are available to U.S. students, including:

- ACT QualityCore,
- Cambridge International General Certificate of Secondary Education,
- Edexcel International General Certificate of Secondary Education,
- College Board AP courses used as diploma programs,
- University of Cambridge Advance International Certificate of Education, and
- International Baccalaureate Diploma Program.

Tucker highlighted some of the differences between board examination systems and typical accountability tests used in the United States. Board examinations are based in curricula as well as standards, designed specifically to capture higher-order thinking skills, and often include information on work done outside of the timed test. Students are expected to study for them, and performance expectations are very clear. In contrast, state accountability tests are generally not curriculum based, and students are not expected to study for them. In his view, students do not always have equal opportunity to study the material on which they will be tested, because the tests tend to cover such broadly defined domains. They do not generally include data on work done outside of the timed test, and they are more effective at capturing basic skills than higher-order thinking skills.

6

Opportunities for Better Assessment

The present moment—when states are moving toward adopting common standards and a federal initiative is pushing them to focus on their assessment systems—seems to present a rare opportunity for improving assessments. Presenters were asked to consider the most promising ways for states to move toward assessing more challenging content and providing better information to teachers and policy makers.

IMPROVEMENT TARGETS

Laurie Wise began with a reminder of the issues that had already been raised: assessments need to support a wide range of policy uses; current tests have limited diagnostic value and are not well integrated with instruction or with interim assessments, and they do not provide optimal information for accountability purposes because they cover only a limited range of what is and should be taught. Improvements are also needed in validity, reliability, and fairness, he said.

For current tests, there is little evidence that they are good indicators of instructional effectiveness or good predictors of students' readiness for subsequent levels of instruction. Their reliability is limited because they are generally targeted to very broad content specifications, and limited progress has been made in assessing all students accurately. Improvements such as computer-based testing and automated scoring need to become both more feasible in the short run and more sustainable in the long run. Wise pointed out that widespread adoption of common standards might help with these challenges in two ways: by pooling their resources, states could get more for the money they spend on assessment, and interstate collaboration is likely to facilitate deeper cognitive analysis of standards and objectives for student performance than is possible with separate standards.

Cost Savings

The question of how much states could save by collaborating on assessment begins with the question of how much they are currently spending. Savings would be likely to be limited to test development, since many per-student costs for administration, scoring, and reporting, would not be affected. Wise discussed an informal survey he had done of development costs (Wise, 2009), which included 15 state testing programs and a few test developers and included only total contract costs, not internal staff costs: the results are shown in Table 6-1.

Perhaps most notable in the data is the wide range in what states are spending, as shown in the minimum and maximum columns. Wise also noted that on average the states surveyed were spending well over $1million annually to develop assessments that require human scoring and $26 per student to score them.

A total of $350 million will be awarded to states through the Race to the Top initiative. That money, plus savings that winning states or consortia could achieve by pooling their resources, together with potential savings from such

TABLE 6-1 Average State Development and Administration Costs by Assessment Type

Assessment Type	N	Mean	S.D.	Min	Max
Annual Development Costs (in thousands of dollars)					
Alternate	9	363	215	100	686
Regular—ECR	13	1,329	968	127	3,600
Regular—MC Only	5	551	387	220	1130
Administrative Cost per Student (in dollars)					
Alternate	9	376	304	40	851
Regular—ECR	16	26	18	4	65
Regular—MC Only	6	3	3	1	9

NOTES: ECR = extended constructed-response tests; Max = maximum cost; MC = multiple-choice tests; Min = minimum cost; N = number; S.D. = standard deviation. Extended constructed-response tests include writing assessments and other tests requiring human scoring using a multilevel scoring rubric. Multiple-choice tests are normally machine scored. Because the results incorporate a number of different contracts, they reflect varying grade levels and subjects, though most included grades 3-8 mathematics and reading.
SOURCE: Wise (2009, p. 4).

new efficiencies as computer delivery, would likely yield for a number of states as much as $13 million each to spend on ongoing development without increasing their own current costs, Wise calculated.

Edward Roeber also examined in detail the question of how a jurisdiction might afford the cost of a new approach to assessment. He began by briefly discussing the idea of a "balanced assessment system," which is one of the top current catch phrases in education policy conversations. He pointed out that users seem to have different ideas of what a coherent system might be. He focused on vertical coherence and said that a balanced system is one that incorporates three broad assessment types: (1) state, national, or even international summative assessments; (2) instructionally relevant interim benchmark assessments; and (3) formative assessments that are embedded in instruction. For him, the key is balance among these three elements, while the current focus is almost entirely on the summative assessments. Interim assessments are not used well, and they tend to simply consist of elements of the large-scale summative assessments. Formative assessments are barely registering as important in most systems. By and large, he said, teachers are not educated about the range of strategies necessary for the continuous process of assessing their students' progress and identifying of areas in which they need more support. The result is that the summative assessments overpower the system.

Others focus on a horizontal balance, Roeber observed, which in practice means that they focus on the skills covered on state assessments. The coherence is between what is included on tests and what is emphasized in classrooms. The emphasis is on preparing students to succeed on the tests, and on providing speedy results, rather than on the quality of the information they provide. Most programs rely too much on multiple-choice questions, which exacerbates the constraining influence of the summative assessments. If states used a broader array of constructed-response and performance items, assessments could have a more positive influence on instruction and could also provide a model for the development of interim assessments that are more relevant to high-quality instruction.

To provide context for discussion of changes states might make in their approaches to assessment, Roeber and his colleagues Barry Topol and John Olson compared the costs of a typical state assessment program with those for a high-quality assessment system (see Topol, Olson, and Roeber, 2010). They hoped to identify strategies for reducing the costs of a higher-quality system. For this analysis, they considered only mathematics, reading, and writing and made the assumption that states would use the common core standards and the same testing contractor. The characteristics of the designs they compared are shown in Tables 6-2 and 6-3. Roeber and his colleagues calculated the cost of a typical assessment program at $20 per student and the cost of a high-quality one at $55 per student (including start-up development costs). Since most states are unlikely to be able to afford a near tripling of their assessment costs,

TABLE 6-2 Numbers of Items of Each Type in Typical Assessment by Design Assessment Type

Subject	Multiple-Choice Items	Short Constructed-Response Items	Extended Constructed-Response Items	Performance Event	Performance Tasks
Mathematics	50	0	2	0	0
Reading	50	0	2	0	0
Writing	10	0	1	0	0
Mathematics—Interim	40	0	0	0	0
English/Language Arts—Interim	40	0	0	0	0

SOURCE: Reprinted from a 2010 paper, "The Cost of New High-Quality Assessments: A Comprehensive Analysis of the Potential Costs for Future State Assessments," with permission by authors Dr. Barry Topol, Dr. John Olson, and Dr. Ed Roeber.

TABLE 6-3 Numbers of Items of Each Type in High-Quality Assessment by Design Assessment Type

Subject	Multiple-Choice Items	Short Constructed-Response Items	Extended Constructed-Response Items	Performance Event	Performance Task
Mathematics	25	2 (1 in grade 3)	2 (0 in grade 3, 1 in grade 4)	2	2 (0 in grade 3, 1 in grade 4)
Reading	25	2 (1 in grades 3 and 4)	2 (1 in grades 3 and 4)	2	1
Writing	10	2 (1 in grades 3 and 4)	2 (1 in grades 3 and 4)	2	0
Mathematics—Interim	25	2	1 (0 in grade 3)	1	1 (0 in grade 3)
English/Language Arts—Interim	25	2	1	1	1

SOURCE: Reprinted from a 2010 paper, "The Cost of New High-Quality Assessments: A Comprehensive Analysis of the Potential Costs for Future State Assessments," with permission by authors Dr. Barry Topol, Dr. John Olson, and Dr. Ed Roeber.

Roeber and his colleagues explored several means of streamlining the cost of the high-quality approach.

First, they considered the savings likely to be possible to a state that collaborated with others, as the states applying for Race the Top funding in consortia plan to do. They calculated that the potential economies of scale would save states an average of $15 per student. New uses of technology, such as online test delivery and automated scoring, would yield immediate savings of $3 to $4 per student, and further savings would be likely with future enhancements of the technology. Roeber observed that some overhead costs associated with converting to a computer-based system would be likely to decline as testing contractors begin to compete more consistently for this work.

They also considered two possible approaches to enlisting teachers to score the constructed-response items. This work might be treated as professional development, in which case there would be no cost beyond that of the usual professional development days. Alternatively, teachers might be paid a stipend ($125 per day per teacher was the figure assumed) for this work. Depending on which approach is taken, the saving would be an additional $10 to $20 per student. Altogether, these measures (assuming teachers are paid for their scoring work) would yield a cost of $21 per student for the high-quality assessment. Moreover, several participants noted, because the experience of scoring is a valuable one for teachers, it is a nonmonetary benefit to the system.

This analysis also showed that the development of a new assessment system would be relatively inexpensive in relation to the total cost: it is the ongoing administration costs that will determine whether states can afford to adopt and sustain new improved assessment systems. Participation in a consortium is likely to yield the greatest costs savings. The bottom line, for Roeber, is that implementing a high-quality assessment system would be possible for most states if they proceed carefully, seeking a balance among various kinds of items with different costs and considering cost-reduction strategies.

Improved Cognitive Analysis

Wise noted that the goal for the common core standards is that they will be better than existing state standards—more crisply defined, clearer, and more rigorous. They are intended to describe the way learning should progress from kindergarten through 12th grade to prepare students for college and work. Assuming that the common standards meet these criteria, states could collaborate to conduct careful cognitive analysis of the skills to be mastered and how they might best be assessed. Working together, states might have the opportunity to explore the learning trajectories in greater detail, for example, in order to pinpoint both milestones and common obstacles to mastery, which could in turn guide decisions about assessment. Clear models for the learning that should take place across years and within grades could support the development of integrated interim assessments, diagnostic assessments, and other tools for meeting assessment goals.

The combination of increased funding for assessments and improved content analyses would, in turn, Wise suggested, support the development of more meaningful reporting. The numerical scales that are now commonly used offer very little meaningful information beyond identifying students above and below an arbitrary cut point. A scale that was linked to detailed learning trajectories (which would presumably be supported by the common standards and elaborated through further analysis) might identify milestones that better convey what students can do and how ready they are for the next stage of learning.

Computer-adaptive testing would be particularly useful in this regard since it provides an easy way to pinpoint an individual student's understanding; in contrast, a uniform assessment may provide almost no information about a student who is performing well above or below grade level. Thus, reports of both short- and long-term growth would be easier, and results could become available more quickly. This faster and better diagnostic information, in turn, could also improve teacher engagement. Another benefit would be increased potential for establishing assessment validity. Test results that closely map onto defined learning trajectories could support much stronger inferences about what students have mastered than are possible with current data, and they could also better support inferences about the relationship between instruction and learning outcomes.

It is clear that common standards can support significant improvements in state assessments, Wise said. The potential cost advantages are apparent. But perhaps more important is that concentrating available brain power and resources on the elaboration of one set of thoughtful standards (as would be possible if a number of states were assessing the same set of standards) would allow researchers to work together for faster progress on assessment development and better data.

IMPLICATIONS FOR SPECIAL POPULATIONS

Much progress has been made in the accurate assessment of special populations—students with disabilities and English language learners (ELLs). Nevertheless, new approaches to assessment may offer the possibility of finding ways to much more accurately measure their learning and to target some of the specific challenges that have hampered past efforts. Robert Linquanti addressed the issues and opportunities innovative assessments present with regard to ELLs, and Martha Thurlow addressed the issues as they relate to students with disabilities.

English Language Learners

Linquanti began by stressing that although ELLs are often referred to as a monolithic entity, they are in fact a very diverse group. This fast-growing group represents 10 percent of the K-12 public school population. Of these 5 million students, 80 percent are Spanish speaking, and approximately 50 percent were born in the United States. They vary in terms of their degree of proficiency in English (and proficiency may vary across each of the four skills of listening, speaking, reading, and writing), the time they have spent in U.S. schools, their level of literacy in their first language, the consistency of their school attendance, and in many social and cultural ways.

Linquanti pointed out that the performance of ELLs on English/language arts is the second most common reason why schools in California (home to many such students) fail to make adequate yearly progress. He also noted that current means of reporting on the performance of ELLs in the National Assessment of Educational Progress (NAEP) skews the picture somewhat, as shown in Figure 6-1. The NAEP reporting does not distinguish among ELLs who have very different levels of academic proficiency. In other words, the data are organized to "create a population that is performing low by definition," Linquanti explained.

It would be better, he said, to have data that provide a finer measure of

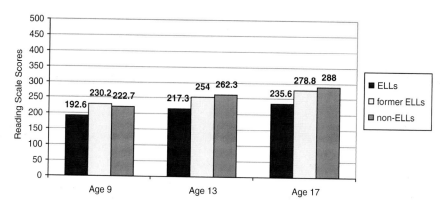

FIGURE 6-1 Average reading scores for current and former ELLs, and non-ELLs on the National Assessment of Educational Progress.
NOTE: ELLs = English language learners.
SOURCE: From Judith Wilde, a paper presented at the 2010 American Educational Research Association annual meeting: *Comparing results of the NAEP Long-Term Trend Assessment: ELLs, Former ELLs, and English-Proficient Students.* Reprinted with permission by the author.

how well these students are doing academically and help to pinpoint the ways their learning is affected by their language proficiency. Though in practice many schools focus on building these students' English skills before addressing their academic needs, that approach is not what the law requires and is not good practice—students need both at the same time.

New approaches to assessment offer several important opportunities for this population, Linquanti said. First, a fresh look at content standards, and particularly at the language demands they will entail, is an opportunity to make more explicit the benchmarks for ELLs to succeed academically. Developing academic language proficiency, he noted, is a key foundation for these students, and the instruction they receive in language support classes (English as a second language, or English language development) is not sufficient for academic success. The sorts of skills being specified more explicitly in the common core standards—for example, analyzing, describing, defining, comparing and contrasting, developing hypotheses, and persuading—are manifested through sophisticated use of language. Some kinds of academic language are discipline specific and others cross disciplines, and making these expectations much more explicit will help teachers identify the skills they need to teach and encourage them to provide students with sufficient opportunities to develop them.

At the same time, the kinds of formative assessment that have been described throughout the workshop will also promote—and enable teachers to monitor—the development of academic language within each subject. If learning targets for language are clearly defined, teachers will be better able to distinguish them from other learning objectives. Linquanti discussed a program called the Formative Language Assessment Records for English Language Learners (FLARE), which identifies specific targets for language learning as well as performance tasks and instructional assessment supports based on them: see Figures 6-2 and 6-3 (see http://flareassessment. org/assessments/learningTargets.aspx [accessed June 2010]). This program, which is now being developed for use in three districts, is designed to actively engage teachers in understanding the language functions required for different kinds of academic proficiency, developing performance tasks, and identifying instructional supports that link to the assessments. Linquanti also welcomed the explicit definitions of language demands for all subjects that are being incorporated in the common core standards, such as those for grades 9-10 in science, which include such tasks as analyzing and summarizing hypotheses and explanations; making inferences; and identifying the relationships among terms, processes, and concepts. If the common core standards are widely adopted, it will be very useful for states to revisit their standards for English language proficiency to ensure that they are well aligned with the academic standards. In Linquanti's view, these language skills must be seen as part of the core, foundational material that students need to master, and teachers

Stage 2

	Level 2: Formulaic		Level 3: Unpacking	
	Language Function	Linguistic Complexity / Vocabulary Usage	Language Function	Linguistic Complexity / Vocabulary Usage
READING	Identify – to recognize, name, or select Summarize – to capture the main point, main idea, or main issue Sequence – to arrange in rank or order	Identify – to recognize, name, or select Summarize – to capture the main point, main idea, or main issue Sequence – to arrange in rank or order	Summarize – to capture the main point, main idea, or main issue Cause/Effect – to identify the origin of an outcome, connect a root to its result, or a product to its trigger	Linguistic Complexity: a variety of sentence lengths of varying linguistic complexity; multiple paragraphs Vocabulary Usage: comprehend specific and some technical language related to the content area; lack of vocabulary may be evident
WRITING	Describe - to explain, give directions, or present details Compare/Contrast – to associate similarities and/or differences	Describe - to explain, give directions, or present details Compare/Contrast – to associate similarities and/or differences	Describe - to explain, give directions, or present details Compare/Contrast – to associate similarities and/or differences in connected sentences and short paragraphs Sequence – to arrange in rank or order and to use transition words to show order	Linguistic Complexity: simple and expanded sentences that show emerging complexity used to provide detail; paragraph level material Vocabulary Usage: general and some specific language related to the content area; lack of vocabulary may be evident

Structure of Genre

Genre	Language Functions	Elements	Text to Read and Produce
Recount or Narrative (to retell, recall accounts or activities)	Sequence, Summary, Cause-effect, Compare-contrast	Setting, situation, complication	• Medium sized documents (e.g., short newspaper articles or letters to the editor) • Paragraph sized statements
Discussion or Argument (to make a point, take a position, present an argument)	Sequence, Summary, Compare-contrast	Statement of issue, reasons for and against, summary of issue	• Multiple paragraphs with supported material, such as drawings and simple charts • Labeled illustrations, diagrams, drawings, pictures, and photographs

FIGURE 6-2 FLARE language functions and genre structures: Levels 2 and 3.

SOURCE: Reprinted with permission from Dr. Gary Cook, principal investigator for FLARE Language Learning Targets, © 2010 Board of Regents of the University of Wisconsin System. FLARE is a 3-year formative assessment grant project (2009-2011) funded by the Carnegie Corporation of New York.

	Stage 2	
	Level 2: Performance Tasks	Level 3: Performance Tasks
READING	Identify the main point in a series of simple sentences or a simple paragraph	Summarize from a short piece of adapted classic or modified text that is, or is not accompanied by supported text (for e.g., in an illustrated poem, a graphic novel, etc.)
	Respond to simple WH-questions about a reading passage (e.g., Who wrote this story?)	Identify characters or events that affect a story's outcome
	Locate key information from simple sentences, paragraphs, or in pictures or graphics	
	Describe the beginning, middle, and end of a story or narrative	
WRITING	Describe familiar people, places, or events	Develop a brief paragraph summarizing the main points in a literary work or informational text
	Describe pictures or graphics related material from literature related topics (e.g., biographies, short stories)	Develop a short paragraph comparing or contrasting information, events, or characters from a literary text
	Connect simple sentences together using conjunctions (e.g., and, but, or)	Sequence events in a story or narrative using transition words
	Describe familiar people, places, or events in phrases or sentences with synonyms or antonyms using word/phrase banks and visuals	

Instructional Assessment Supports

Sensory: Dictionary, illustrations, diagrams, pictures, manipulatives, real-life objects, recordings, videos, magazines/newspapers, broadcasts, physical activity

Graphical: Graphic organizers, timelines, charts

Interactive: In native language groupings, pairs or with partners, triads or small groups, or whole groups; with mentors, on the Internet w/ supportive software

FIGURE 6-3 FLARE performance tasks and instructional assessment supports: Levels 2 and 3.
SOURCE: Reprinted with permission from Dr. Gary Cook, principal investigator for FLARE Language Learning Targets, © 2010 Board of Regents of the University of Wisconsin System. FLARE is a 3-year formative assessment grant project (2009-2011) funded by the Carnegie Corporation of New York.

need to be guided in incorporating these targets into their instruction. This greater clarity will help teachers distinguish whether poor performance is the result of insufficient language skills to demonstrate the other skills or knowledge that a student has, lack of those other knowledge and skills, unnecessarily complex language in the assessment, or other factors (such as cultural difference, dialect variation, or rater misinterpretation).

Above all, Linquanti stressed, it is critical not to treat the participation of ELLs in new, innovative assessments as an afterthought—the role of language in every aspect of the system should be a prime concern throughout design and development. This point is also especially important for any high-stakes uses of assessments. "We have to calibrate the demands of the performance with the provisions of support—and make sure we are clarifying and monitoring the expectations we have for kids," he said.

Students with Disabilities

Martha Thurlow observed that many of the issues Linquanti had raised also apply to students with disabilities, and she agreed that the opportunity to include all students from the beginning, rather than retrofitting a system to accommodate them, is invaluable. She stressed that the sorts of assessments being described at the workshop already incorporate the key to assessing students with disabilities: not to devise special instruments for particular groups, but to have a system that is flexible enough to measure a wide range of students.

She noted that, like ELLs, students with disabilities are not well understood as a group. Figure 6-4 shows the proportions of students receiving special education services who have been classified in each of 12 categories of disability; Thurlow pointed out that approximately 85 percent of them do not have any intellectual impairment. Moreover, she noted, even students with severe cognitive disabilities can learn much more than many people realize, as recent upward trends in theoir performance on NAEP suggest.

Thurlow noted that universal design, as described by the National Accessible Reading Assessment Projects of the U.S. Department of Education (Accessibility Principles for Reading (see http://www.narap.info/ [accessed June 2010]), means considering all students beginning with the design of standards and continuing throughout the design, field testing, and implementation of an assessment.[1] Accommodations and alternate assessments that support valid and reliable measurement of the performance of students with disabilities are key elements of this approach. However, developing effective, fair accommodations and alternate

---

[1]Additional information about universal design can be found at the website of the National Center on Educational Outcomes (see http://www.cehd.umn.edu/nceo/ [accessed June 2010]).

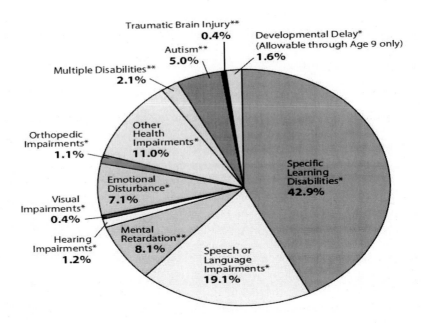

FIGURE 6-4 Students who receive special education services by disability category. SOURCE: Reprinted with permission from the National Center for Learning Disabilities' publication, *Challenging Change: How Schools and Districts Are Improving the Performance of Special Education Students* © 2008.

assessments that are based on achievement levels modified to fit the capacities of student with various disabilities remains a challenge.

Lack of access to curriculum and instruction also continues to confound interpretation of assessment results for this group, Thurlow added, and to limit expectations for what they can master. Specialists and researchers continue to struggle with questions about what it means for students with different sorts of disabilities to have access to curriculum at their grade levels.

These are some of the challenges that exist as possibilities for new kinds of assessment are contemplated, Thurlow said. The opportunity to have more continuous monitoring of student progress that could come with a greater emphasis on formative assessment, for example, would clearly be a significant benefit for students with disabilities, in her view. Similarly, computer-adaptive testing is an attractive possibility, though it will be important to explore whether the algorithms that guide the generation of items account for unusual patterns of knowledge or thinking. Above all, Thurlow stressed, "we have to remember that students with disabilities can learn . . . and take a principled approach to their inclusion in innovative assessments."

TECHNOLOGY

Randy Bennett began by noting that new technology is already being used in K-12 assessments. Computerized adaptive testing is being administered in thousands of districts at every grade level to assess reading, mathematics, science, and languages. At the national level, NAEP will soon offer an online writing assessment for the 8th and 12th grades, and the Programme for International Student Assessment (PISA) exams now include a computerized reading assessment that relies on local schools' infrastructure. So technology-based assessment is no longer a "wild idea," Bennett observed. Because it is likely that technology will soon become a central force in assessment, he said, it is important to ensure that its development be guided by substantive concerns, rather than efficiency concerns. "If we focus exclusively, or even primarily, on efficiency concerns," he argued, "we may end up with nothing more than the ability to make arguably mediocre tests faster, cheaper, and in greater numbers." Increasing efficiency may be a worthy short-term goal, but only as a means to reach the goal of substantively driven technology-based innovation.

Moreover, he said, current standards cannot by themselves provide enough guidance for the design of assessments in a way that is consistent with the results of the research on learning discussed earlier in the workshop (see Chapter 2). Two key needs, Bennett said, are: competency models that identify the components of proficiency in a domain (that is, key knowledge, processes, strategies, or habits of mind) and also describe how those competencies work together to facilitate skilled performance; and learning progressions that identify the ways learning develops sequentially (see Chapter 2). Figure 6-5 shows how technology fits in a model of coherent instruction and assessment.

With that model in mind, Bennett identified 11 propositions that he believes should guide the use of technology in assessment, goals.

1. Technology should be used to give students more substantively meaningful tasks than might be feasible through traditional approaches, by presenting rich content about which they can be asked to reason, read, write, or do other tasks. He offered as an example an item developed for the Educational Testing Service's CBAL (Cognitively Based Assessment of, for, and as Learning). In this task on the topic of electronic waste (discarded electronic devices, which often contain heavy metals and other pollutants), which is designed to be conducted over days or weeks, depending on how it is integrated into other instruction, students are asked to perform tasks that include: listening to an online radio news report and taking notes on its content; evaluating websites that contain relevant information; reading articles about the topic and writing responses and other pieces; using a graphic organizer to manage information from different sources; and working collaboratively to develop an informational poster. Many of the tasks are primarily formative assessments, but a subset can be used to provide summative data. The cost of presenting this range of material on paper

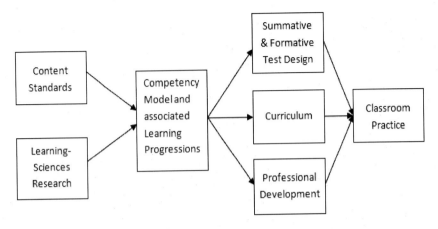

FIGURE 6-5 Model of a coherent system: Where technology fits.
SOURCE: Reprinted with permission from the Educational Testing Service © 2010.

would be prohibitive, and the logistics of managing it would be a significant challenge not only for schools and teachers, but even for the students who interact with the materials. But more important than the convenience, Bennett said, is that the complexity of the materials makes it possible to engage students in higher-order skills and also to build their skills and knowledge.

2. Technology-based assessment should model good instructional practice for teachers and learning practice for students by including the tools that proficient performers typically use and reflecting the ways they represent knowledge. Such tasks should encourage the habits of mind common to experts in the domain being tested. In another example from the electronic waste task, students work with an interactive screen to locate, prioritize, and organize information, to develop an outline, and to draft an essay. They have the option of selecting from a variety of organizing strategies. They may be given details and asked to develop general statements from them or given such statements and asked to locate and fill in relevant supporting details. The focus is on modeling the use of criteria to help students think critically in an online context, where the amount of information is far greater and the quality far more variable than they are likely to find in their classrooms or local libraries. Thus, the tasks both teach methods of organizing and writing and reinforce concepts, such as criteria for evaluating the quality of sources.

3. Technology should be used to assess important (higher- and lower-order) competencies that are not easily measured by conventional means. Examples could include having students read orally; use simulations of dynamic systems to interpret evidence, discover relationships, infer causes, or pose solutions; use spreadsheet for mathematical modeling of complex problem situations;

read and write on the computer in a nonlinear task; or digitally document the products of an extended project.

4. Technology should be used to measure students' skills at using technology for problem solving. Successful performance in advanced academic settings and in workplaces will require skill and flexibility in using technology, so this domain should become part of what schools measure.

5. Technology should be used to collect student responses that can support more sophisticated interpretation of their knowledge and skills than is typical with traditional tests. For example, the time taken in answering questions can indicate how automatic basic skills have become or the degree of motivations a student has to answer correctly. Tracking of other aspects of students' responses and decisions may also illuminate their problem-solving processes. Using a sample item, Bennett showed how assessors could evaluate the search terms students used and the relevance of the web pages they chose to visit, which were related to the quality of their constructed responses.

6. Technology should be used to make assessments fairer for all students, including those with disabilities and ELLs. Incorporating vocabulary links for difficult words in an assessment that is not measuring vocabulary, offering alternate representations of information (e.g., text, speech, verbal descriptions of illustrations), or alternate questions measuring the same skills are all tools that can yield improved measures of students' learning.

7. Adaptive testing could be enhanced to assess a fuller range of competencies than it currently does. Current adaptive tests rely on multiple-choice items because real-time scoring of constructed responses has not been feasible, but automatic scoring is now an option. Students could also be routed to appropriately difficult extended constructed-response items, which would then be scored after the test administration.

8. Technology can support more frequent measurement, so that information collected over time for formative purposes can be aggregated for summative purposes. When assessment tasks are substantive, model good learning and teaching practice, and provide useful interim information, they can offer better information for decision making than a single end-of-year test.

9. Technology can be used to improve the quality of scoring. Online human scoring makes it possible for monitors to track the performance of raters and flag those who are straying from rubrics or scoring too quickly given the complexity of the responses. As noted earlier, he said, progress has also been made with automated scoring of short text responses, essays, mathematics equations or other numerical or graphic responses, and spoken language. However, Bennett cautioned, automated scoring can easily be misused, if, for example, it rewards proxies for good performance, such as essay length. Thus, he advocated that the technology's users probe carefully to be sure that the program rewards key competencies rather than simply predicting the operational behavior of human scorers.

10. Technology can allow assessors to report results quickly and provide useful information for instructional decision making. Classroom-level information and common errors can be reported immediately, for example, and other results (such as those that require human scoring) can be phased in as they become available. Electronic results can also be structured to link closely to the standards they are measuring, for example, by showing progress along a learning progression. The results could also be linked to a competency model, instructional materials suitable for the next steps a student needs to take, exemplars of good performance at the next level, and so forth. The information could be presented in a hierarchical web page format, so users can see essential information quickly and dig for details as they need them.

11. Technology can be used to help teachers and students understand the characteristics of good performance by participating in online scoring. Students could score their own or others' anonymous work as an instructional exercise. Teachers may gain formative information from scoring their own students' work and that of other students as part a structured, ongoing professional development experience.

Bennett acknowledged that pursuing these 11 goals would pose a number of challenges. First, current infrastructure is not yet sufficient to support efficient, secure testing of large groups of students in the ways he described, and innovative technology-based assessments are very costly to develop. Because students bring a range of computer skills to the classroom, it is possible that those with weaker skills would be less able to demonstrate their content skills and knowledge, and their scores would underestimate them. Many of the stimuli that computer graphics make possible could be inaccessible to students with certain disabilities. Interactive assessments also make it possible to collect a range of information, but researchers have not yet identified reliable ways to extract meaningful information from all of these data.

None of these issues is intractable, Bennett argued, but they are likely to make the promise of computer-based assessment difficult to fulfill in the near term. Nevertheless, he suggested, "if you don't think big enough you may well succeed at things that in the long run really weren't worth achieving."

State Perspectives

Wendy Pickett provided perspective from Delaware, a state that has been a good place to practice new technology because of its small size. Delaware, which has approximately 10,000 students per grade, is currently phasing in a new online, adaptive system. It will include benchmark interim assessments as well as end-of-course assessments, and the state has positioned itself to move forward quickly with other options, such as computerized teacher evaluations, as they consider the implications for them of the Race to the Top awards, adoption of the common core standards, and other developments.

She noted that, as in many states, there are pressures to meet numerous goals with the state assessment, including immediate scores, individualized diagnostic information, and summative evaluations. At the same time, the landscape at the local, state, and national levels is changing rapidly, she observed: developing the new assessment has felt like "flying an airplane while redesigning the wings and the engine."

However, the state's small size makes it easy to maintain good communication among the 19 districts and 18 charter schools. All the district superintendents can meet one or twice a month, and technology has helped them share information quickly. The state has also had a tradition of introducing new tests to the public through an open-house structure, in which samples are available at malls and restaurants. The state will do the same with the new online test, Pickett said, using mobile computer labs—and plans to use the labs to introduce state legislators to the new technology as well.

Among the features Delaware is incorporating in its new assessment are items in which students will create graphs on the screen and use online calculators, rulers, and formula sheets. The state is working to guide teachers to ensure that all their students are familiar with the operations they will need to perform for the assessment tasks. The state also has a data warehouse that makes information easily accessible and allows users to pursue a variety of links. The danger, she cautioned, is that "you can slice and dice things in so many ways that you can overinterpret" the information, and she echoed others in highlighting the importance of training for teachers in data analysis. Pickett closed with the observation that "the technology can help us be more transparent, but we owe it to all our stakeholders to be very clear about our goals and how we are using technology to accomplish them."

Tony Alpert focused on the needs of states that have not yet "bridged the technology gap," noting how difficult it is to make the initial move from paper-based to technology-based assessment. He noted the experiences of Delaware, Hawaii, and other states that are farther along can be invaluable in highlighting lessons learned and sensible ways to phase in the change. In his view, the most important step is to provide professional development not just to teachers, but also to state-level staff so that they will be equipped to build and support the system. States' experiences with logistical challenges, such as monitoring the functioning of an application that is being used with multiple operating systems, could save others a lot of headaches as well.

Alpert also commented on Bennett's view that assessment tasks can be engaging and educational even as they provide richer information about students' knowledge and skills. He observed that somehow the most interesting items tend to get blocked by the sensitivity and bias committees, perhaps in part because they may favor students with particular knowledge. It will be an ongoing challenge, in his view, to continue to develop complex and engaging tasks that will be fair to every student.

Participants noted other challenges, including the fast pace at which new devices are being developed. Students may quickly adapt to new technologies, but assessment developers will need to be mindful of ways to design for evolving screen types and other variations in hardware, because images may render very differently on future devices than on those currently available, for example. Other challenges with compatibility were noted, but most participants agreed that the key is to proceed in incremental steps toward a long-term goal that is grounded in objectives for teaching and learning.

7

Making Use of Assessment Information

At the heart of any plan for improving assessment is the goal of obtaining information about what students have and have not learned that can be used to help them improve their learning, to guide their teachers, and to support others who make decisions about their education.

USING ASSESSMENTS TO GUIDE INSTRUCTION

Linda Darling-Hammond explored how assessment information can be used to guide instruction—for example, by providing models of good instruction and high-quality student work, diagnostic information, and evidence about the effectiveness of curricula and instruction. As she had discussed earlier, when rich assessment tasks are embedded in the curriculum, they can serve multiple purposes more effectively than can current accountability tests and can influence instruction in positive ways. She provided several examples of tasks that engage students in revealing their thinking and reasoning and that elicit complex knowledge and skills.

A performance task developed for an Ohio end-of-course exam, for example, requires mathematical analysis and modeling, as well as sophisticated understanding of ratio and proportion. It presents a scenario in which a woman needs to calculate how much money she saved in heating bills after purchasing insulation, taking into account variation in weather from year to year. To answer the questions, students must do tasks that include Internet research to gain contextual information, calculating the cost-effectiveness of the insulation, and writing a written summary of their findings and conclusions. They are also asked to devise a generalized method of comparison using set formulas and to create a pamphlet for gas company customers explaining this tool. Some of the questions that are part of this assessment are shown in Box 7-1.

This sort of task, Darling-Hammond explained, is engaging for students in part because it elicits complex knowledge and skills. It also reveals to teachers the sorts of thinking and reasoning of which each student is capable. It does so in part because it was developed based on an understanding of the learning progressions characteristic of this area of study and of students' cognitive development. Because of these characteristics of the assessment, scoring and analyzing the results are valuable learning opportunities for teachers.[1] Darling-Hammond stressed that in several other places (e.g., Finland, Sweden, and the Canadian province Alberta) teachers are actively engaged in the development of assessment tasks, as well as scoring and analysis, which makes it easier for them to see and forge the links between what is assessed and what they teach. In general, she suggested, "the conversation about curriculum and instruction in this country is deeply impoverished in comparison to the conversation that is going on in other countries." For example, the idea that comparing test scores obtained at two different points in time is sufficient to identify student growth is simplistic, in her view. Much more useful would be a system that identifies numerous benchmarks along a vertical scale—a learning continuum—and incorporates thoughtful means of using it to measure students' progress. This sort of data could then to be combined with other data about students and teachers to provide a richer picture of instruction and learning.

Darling-Hammond noted that technology greatly expands the opportunities for this sort of assessment. In addition to delivering the assessments and providing rapid feedback, it can be used to provide links to instructional materials and other resources linked to the standards being assessed. It can be used to track data about students' problem-solving strategies or other details of their responses and make it easy to aggregate results in different ways for different purposes. It can also facilitate human scoring, in part be making it possible for teachers to participate without meeting in a central location. Technology can also make it possible for students to compile digital records of their performance on complex tasks that could be used to demonstrate their progress or readiness for further study in a particular area or in a postsecondary institution. Such an assessment system could also make it easier for policy makers to understand student performance: for example, they could see not just abstract scores, but exemplars of student work, at the classroom, school, or district level.

---

[1] For detailed descriptions of learning progressions in English/language arts, mathematics, and other subjects, Darling-Hammond pointed participants to the website of England's Qualifications and Curriculum Authority (http://www.qcda.gov.uk/ [accessed June 2010]). Assessment tasks are developed from theses descriptions and teachers use them both to identify how far students have progressed on various dimensions and also to report their progress to others and for instruction planning purposes.

BOX 7-1
Ohio Performance Assessment Project
"Heating Degree Days" Task

Based on Ms. Johnson's situation and some initial information, begin to research "heating degree days" on the Internet:

(1) Assess the cost-effectiveness of Ms. Johnson's new insulation and window sealing. In your assessment, you must do the following:

- Compare Ms. Johnson's gas bills from January 2007 and January 2008.
- Explain Ms. Johnson's savings after the insulation and sealing.
- Identify circumstances under which Ms. Johnson's January 2008 gas bill would have been at least 10% less than her January 2007 bill.
- Decide if the insulation and sealing work on Ms Johnson's house was cost-effective and provide evidence for this decision.

(2) Create a short pamphlet for gas company customers to guide them in making decisions about increasing the energy efficiency of their homes. The pamphlet must do the following:

- List the quantities that customers need to consider in assessing the cost-effectiveness of energy efficiency measures.
- Generalize the method of comparison used for Ms. Johnson's gas bills with a set of formulas, and provide an explanation of the formulas.
- Explain to gas customers how to weigh the cost of energy efficiency measures with savings on their gas bills.

SOURCE: Reprinted with permission from Linda Darling-Hammond on behalf of Stanford University School Redesign Network, Using Assessment to Guide Instruction: "Ohio Performance Assessment Project 'Heating Degree Days' Task." Copyright 2009 by Ohio Department of Education.

SUPPORTING TEACHERS

Many teachers seem to have difficulty using assessment information to plan instruction, Margaret Heritage observed, but if they don't know how to do this, "they are really not going to have the impact on student learning that is the goal of all this investment on effort." A number of studies have documented this problem, examining teachers' use of assessments designed to inform instruction in reading, mathematics, and science (Herman et al., 2006; Heritage et al., 2009; Heritage, Jones, and White, 2010; Herman, Osmubdson, and Silver, 2010).

There are a number of possible reasons for this difficulty, Heritage noted. Perhaps most important is that preservice education in the United States does not, as a rule, leave teachers with an expectation that assessment is a tool to support their work. Figure 7-1 illustrates the kinds of professional knowledge that teachers need in order to make use of the rich information that sophisticated assessments can provide, presented as a set of interacting cogs.

First, teachers need to have a complex enough understanding of the structure of the discipline they are teaching to have a clear cognitive road map in which to fit assessment information. This understanding of how ideas develop from rudimentary forms into more sophisticated conceptual frameworks is the foundation for the learning maps discussed earlier (see Chapter 2) and is also key to teachers' work. There are many teachers who do have this knowledge, Heritage stressed, but many more who do not. Teachers also need sufficient knowledge of how students learn within a domain—pedagogical content knowledge. Understanding of how a particular concept or skill is learned can help teachers plan instruction that meets their students' needs. Finally, teachers

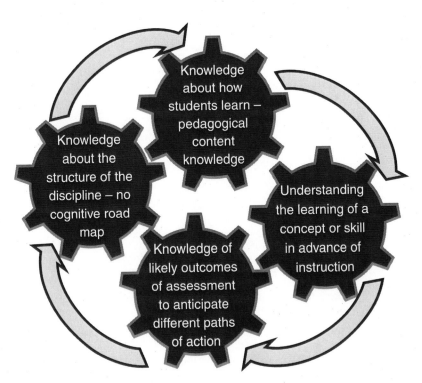

FIGURE 7-1 Knowledge that teachers need to utilize assessments.
SOURCE: Heritage (2010, slide #3).

need to have both the time and the experience to consider in advance the likely outcomes of an assessment so that they can plan possible courses of action.

Another way of thinking about how teachers might use high-quality assessment results is to consider both what both learners and teachers ought to do with the results, Heritage said. Research on the differences between novices and experts (see National Research Council, 2001) shows that experts not only possess more information, they also have complex structures for their knowledge that guide them is assimilating new information and using their knowledge in a variety of ways. Thus, learners need not only to accumulate discrete knowledge, but also to develop increasingly sophisticated conceptual frameworks for the knowledge and skills they are acquiring. They also need to use metacognitive strategies to guide their own learning—that is, to monitor and assess their own progress and develop strategies for making progress.

How can a teacher support this learning? One way is to structure each student's classroom experiences so that they focus on learning goals that fit the progress that student has already made, and Heritage stressed how important it is for teachers to understand that students do not "all learn at the same pace, in the same way, at the same time." Ideally, teachers will be equipped to recognize "ripening structures," areas where students are just ready to take a next step. Providing feedback to students is how teachers can guide students, and assessment information can provide the material for very precise feedback. Particularly important, Heritage said, is that assessment results can provide not just retrospective views of what students have already learned, but clear, specific pointers to where they should go next. Table 7-1 shows some of the responses students and teachers might have to rich assessment information, as well as some ways that assessments can support those responses.

How then, might the public school system best support teachers? Heritage noted that all aspects of the education system in the United Kingdom, where she spent much of her career, provide better support for teachers than do the national, state, and local systems in the United States, though it is worth remembering that the United States is much larger and delegates most educational control to local districts. Nevertheless, for her, the first place to look for changes is higher education. Too many graduating U.S. teachers are not well prepared, particularly in the ways described above, and Heritage highlighted several kinds of knowledge teachers need:

- models of how students' thinking and skills develop within a discipline and across disciplines;
- understanding of the kinds of challenges to learning students face in a discipline;
- understanding of the interdependence of teaching and learning and emerging developmental processes;
- deep pedagogical content knowledge; and

- understanding of ways to involve students in learning and assessment, and of how to evidence of their understanding in the course of a lesson—along with strategies for responding to their findings.

Teachers also need a variety of resources in order to work effectively, Heritage noted. First, they need sound assessments that are "worth teaching to" and cover a range of performance. Descriptions of students' learning trajectories developed through research (such as the cognitive maps earlier; see Chapter 2) are critical, in Heritage's view. From her perspective the common core standards are "skeletal" in this respect. If clear descriptions of learning progressions were available, assessments could be linked to clear descriptions of performance goals and of what particular levels of competence look like. Teachers also need an array of resources that support them in interpreting information and acting on it. England's Qualifications and Curriculum Authority (see footnote 1) is one example; other countries also provide specific resources built around the assessment and the curriculum. "It amazes me that we don't have a Smithsonian of exemplary teacher practices," she added.

Heritage said that U.S. teachers are also not given nearly enough time for the reflection and planning that are essential to thoughtful use of information and instructional planning. U.S. teachers spend an average of 1,130 contract hours in the classroom, she noted; in contrast, the average for countries in the

TABLE 7-1 Possible Student and Teacher Responses to Assessment Information

Learner	Teacher	Assessment to Support Teacher Learning
• Construct new concepts based on current and prior knowledge.	• Structure new experiences within the ZPD that build on previous "ripening" learning.	• Indicate actual and potential development (retrospective and prospective).
• Develop integrated knowledge structures (schema).	• Engage students in interactions and activity to create networks structured around key ideas.	• Embody learning practices (assessment as teaching).
• Apply knowledge to new situations.		• Integrate cognition and context.
• Use metacognitive strategies.	• Provide feedback.	• Make students' thinking visible.
	• Support metacognitive activity and self-regulation.	• Locate learning status in the larger landscape.

Organisation for Economic Co-operation and Development is 803 hours for primary teachers and 674 hours for upper secondary teachers. But perhaps most important, she said, is that U.S. teachers are consistently asked to implement programs that have been devised by someone else, rather than to study the practice of their vocation.

Karin Hess drew on her involvement with several research programs to sketch a view of strategies for supporting teachers in using assessment results. One, the Center for Collaborative Education (see http://www.cce.org/ [accessed June 2010]), has focused on ways to incorporate performance assessment into accountability programs for Massachusetts middle and high schools. The professional development approach includes teacher workshop time to participate in developing a standards-based assessment and for analyzing student work. Another, the Hawaii Progress Maps, has focused on documenting learning progression and formative assessment practices (Hess, Kurizaki, and Holt, 2009). As part of the project, researchers asked teachers to identify struggling students and to track their strategies with those students throughout the year. Teachers had access to a profile that shows the benchmarks and learning progressions for each grade, which they could use in documenting the students' progress.

From these and other projects that have explored the use of learning progressions in formative assessment, Hess had several observations. First, she emphasized that learning progressions are very specific, research-based description of how students develop specific skills in a specified domain. She noted that curricular sequences and scopes and other documents intended to serve the same purpose are often not true learning progressions, in that they do not describe the way students develop competence in a discipline. For example, she noted, it is all too easy, for a curriculum document to include skills that may be important but that are beyond the capacity of most students at the level in which they are included.

Heritage said she has also found that teachers who engage in this work alter their perceptions about students, as well as their own teaching practice, and they came to better understand the standards to which they are teaching. Teachers in the Hawaii project, for example, found that they had to get to know their students better in order to place them properly on a learning continuum, and they incorporated that thinking into their assessment designs. The teachers also said that they began to focus on what their students could do, rather than on what they could not do, in part because they had a clearer understanding of the "big picture," a more complete understanding of how proficiency in a particular area would look.

PRACTITIONERS' PERSPECTIVES

Teri Siskind offered some of the lessons educators in South Carolina have learned through several projects focused on improving teacher quality. In one project, the state experimented with using trained assessment coaches to provide personalized feedback to teachers to help improve their use of assessment data: however, the results were similar to those achieved with untrained facilitators. In general, the teachers did improve in their ability to develop tasks and interpret the results, but there was no clear evidence that these improvements led to improved student achievement. That study also showed that teachers did not understand the state's standards well, although the reason may lie more with the standards themselves than with teachers.

Another project was a pilot science assessment using hands-on tasks developed by WestEd (a nonprofit agency that develops assessment materials and provides technical assistance to districts, states, and other entities) that was tailored to South Carolina's standards. The project showed that the teachers' participation in scoring the tasks was very beneficial, because it both improved their understanding of student work and engaged them in thinking about the science concepts the standards were targeting. The project also found that teachers were willing and able to develop assessments of this type. However, as with the other project, Siskind noted, there was no subsequent evidence of effects on student performance.

South Carolina is also collaborating with the Dana Center and education company Agile Mind on a 3-year, classroom-embedded training effort called the Algebra project. This project, which is being developed incrementally, involves summer training for teachers and support during the school year in mathematics and science. The project is so small that Siskind described its effects thus far as "little ripples in a vast ocean," but she emphasized that the state hopes to develop better systems for evaluating these sorts of projects. She hopes they will improve the capacity to examine measures of teacher performance, fidelity of implementation, sustainability, and results—and also to better track which students have been exposed to teachers who have received particular supports. Unfortunately, the state has lost funding for many of these programs.

South Carolina's Department of Education also requested funding from the legislature to support the development and implementation of a comprehensive formative assessment system. However, the legislation that resulted diverged significantly from what had been requested, though it incorporates some elements. Siskind said districts have had mixed reactions to some of the changes suggested, noting that "some things that are lovingly embraced when they are voluntary turn evil when they are mandated."

Peg Cagle, a long-time middle school mathematics teacher in California, began with the observation that "a good assessment system would buttress, not batter, classroom teachers." She noted that she was extremely impressed by the visionary ideas presented at the workshop, but that "the most visionary design coupled with myopic implementation is not going to improve teaching or learning." At present, she said, the California state assessment system has very high stakes for teachers but not for students, so, in effect, teachers are rewarded for their success at persuading students to care about the results. Teachers and principals resort to stunts to capture students' attention—which is hardly the purpose of assessment, she cautioned. If an assessment system is easily gamed, she added, it really is not a measure of what students know, but of what they have learned to show.

Cagle also contrasted the optimism in the discussions of the potential that innovative assessments offer and the current state of teacher morale around the country. The punitive nature of assessment is a significant factor in their low morale, in her view. While she strongly favors looking for ways to make sure the teaching force is of the highest quality, she believes that current means of judging teachers do not reflect the complexity of the work they do. The hardest part of the job, she added, is identifying the misconceptions that are impeding students' progress in order to address them effectively. Current assessments rarely provide that kind of information, but it is what teachers need most. Moreover, the veil of secrecy surrounding the state's assessment is not a service to teachers or students. Cagle only sees the assessments her students take if one is absent, leaving a book free during the test for her to examine—and even that examination is officially prohibited. The limited number of items released after the testing are not sufficient to help her understand what it is the students did not understand or why.

A good assessment system, Cagle said, would focus less on statistical information and more on opportunities for teachers to engage in thinking about student work. Current assessments, by and large, she argued, reflect "a tragically impoverished view of what public education is supposed to provide."

AGGREGATING INFORMATION FROM DIFFERENT SOURCES

Laurie Wise returned to the idea of a coherent system, a term that implies disparate, but interrelated, parts that work together. He focused on how it might be possible to aggregate disparate elements to provide summative information that meets a range of purposes.

He turned first to why it is important to aggregate separate pieces, rather than just relying on an end-of-the-year test—a point stressed repeatedly across the two workshops. He summarized much of the discussion by noting that a system of assessments that captures information of different kinds at multiple points during instruction can provide deeper, more timely information that can be used formatively as well as summatively and can establish a much closer link between curriculum and instruction and assessment. It also offers opportunities for the assessment of complex, higher-order thinking and perhaps for measuring teacher and school effectiveness, as well.

It is still important to sum up this information, though, for at least three reasons. In addition to obtaining rich profiles of diagnostic information, educators need information they can use to make decisions about students, such as whether they are ready to advance to the next grade or course or to graduate form high school. Schools and districts also need input regarding teacher performance, and evidence of student learning is an important kind of input, though Wise cautioned that other sorts of information are also very important. Systems also need this sort of information in order to make decisions about schools.

Given that aggregation is useful, there are a number of ways it might be done, Wise suggested. Simplest, perhaps, would be to administer the same assessment several times during the year and assign students their highest score, though this approach would be limited in the content it could cover, among other disadvantages. Through-course assessment, where different tests are administered at several points during the year, is anther possibility, of which there are several versions. One version is end-of-unit tests, which allows for deeper coverage of the material in each part of the year's instruction. This approach could be supplemented by an end-of-course assessment. Another possibility is cumulative tests, in which each test addresses all of the content covered up to that point. This model would allow students to demonstrate that they have overcome weaknesses (e.g., lack of knowledge) that were evident in earlier assessments.

Considering the nature of reading comprehension suggests another sort of model, Wise said. Reading is not taught in discrete chunks, but rather developed over time with increasingly complex stimuli and challenges, so the separate component model does not fit this domain well. (Wise noted that the same might be true of other domains.) Instead, the goal for assessment would be to test skill levels with increasing subtlety at several points during the year. Doing so would make it possible to measure growth through the year and also provide a summative measure at the end. As with the other models, it would be possible to assign differing weights to different components of the assessment in calculating the summative score. The design of the assessment and the weighting should reflect the nature of the subject, the grade level, and other factors, Wise added.

There is some tension between the formative and summative purposes of testing, even in these models. For example, Wise noted, having students score their own work and having teachers score their students' work is an advantage in formative assessment but a disadvantage in summative assessment. These models could be devised to permit some of both, thus allowing teachers to see how closely their formative results map onto summative results. For example, each of the tests administered throughout the year could include both summative and formative portions, some of which might be scored by the teacher and some of which might be scored externally.

Another approach is the one that is common in many college courses, in which a final grade is based on a final exam, a mid-term exam, and a paper, with different weights for each. More broadly, Wise noted, it could encompass any combination of test plus some portfolio of work that would be scored according to a common rubric. Relative weights could be determined based on a range of factors. Testing could also include group tasks, for example, in order to measure skills valued by employers, such as collaboration. In this approach, group scores would be combined with individual scores, and Wise note that technology might offer options for scoring individual contributions to group results. Results could also be collected at the school level, for other purposes.

Wise also considered the way alternate models of testing might be used to provide information about teacher effectiveness. In the current school-level accountability system, teachers are highly motivated to work together to make sure that all students in the school succeed because the school is evaluated on the basis of how all students do. If, instead, data were aggregated by teacher, there might be a perverse incentive for greater competition among teachers—which is not likely to be good for students. One solution would be to incorporate other kinds of information about teachers, as is done in many other employment settings. For example, teacher ratings could include not only student achievement data, but also principal and peer ratings on such factors as contributions to the school as a whole and the learning environment, innovations, and so forth. Such a system might also be used diagnostically, to help identify areas in which teachers need additional support and development.

Wise had three general recommendations for assessment:

1. Assessments should closely follow, but also lead, the design of instruction.
2. Assessments should provide timely, actionable information, as well as summative information needed for evaluation.
3. Aggregation of summative information should support the validity of intended interpretations. With a complex system—as opposed to a single assessment—it is possible to meet multiple purposes in a valid manner.

"There is potentially great value to a more continuous assessment system incorporating different types of measures—even to the extremes of portfolios and group tasks," Wise concluded, and the flexibility such an approach offers for meeting a variety of goals is perhaps its greatest virtue."

8

Challenges of Developing New Assessments

The many opportunities that innovative, coherent assessment systems seem to offer were clearly inspiring to many participants, but the challenges of developing a new generation of assessments that meet the goals in a technically sound manner were also apparent. Rebecca Zwick provided an overview of some of the technical issues, and Ron Hambleton looked in depth at issues related to ensuring the student performance can be compared across states.

TECHNICALLY SOUND INNOVATIVE ASSESSMENTS

"We ask a lot of our state assessments these days," noted Zwick, and she enumerated some of the many goals that had been mentioned. Tests should be valid and reliable and support comparisons at least within consortiums and across assessment years. They should also be fair to ethnic, gender, and socioeconomic groups, as well as to English language learners and students with disabilities. They should be conducive to improved teaching and useful for cognitive diagnosis. They should be developmentally appropriate and well aligned with standards, curriculum, and instruction, and they should be engaging to students. They should also provide data quickly enough to be useful in current lessons, according to the specifications in the Race to the Top grant application information.[1]

---

[1]For details, see "Proposed Regulations on the Race to the Top (RTT) fund of the American Recovery and Reinvestment Act of 2009" (74 Fed. Reg. 37804, Section IV, p. 37811), proposed July 2009.

How easily might innovative assessments used for summative, account-ability purposes meet these goals? First, Zwick observed, many aspects of the current vision of innovative assessment (e.g., open-ended questions, essays, hands-on science problems, computer simulations of real-world problems, and portfolios of student work) were first proposed in the early 1990s, and in some cases as far back as the work of E.F. Lindquist in the early 1950s (Lindquist, 1951; also see Linn et al., 1991). She cited as an example a science test that was part of the 1989 California Assessment Program. The assessment consisted of 15 hands-on tasks for 6th graders, set up in stations, which included develop-ing a classification system for leaves and testing lake water to see why fish were dying (see Shavelson et al., 1993). The students conducted experiments and prepared written responses to questions. The responses were scored using a rubric developed by teachers.

This sort of assessment is intrinsically appealing, Zwick observed, but it is important to consider a few technical questions. Do the tasks really measure the intended higher-order skills? Procedural complexity does not always guarantee cognitive complexity, she noted, and, as with multiple-choice items, teaching to the test can undermine the value of its results. If students are drilled on the topics of the performance assessments, such as geometry proofs or writ-ing 20-minute essays, it may be that, when tested, they would not need to use higher-order thinking skills to do these tasks because they have memorized how to do them.

Another question is whether the results can be generalized across tasks. Can a set of hands-on science tasks be devised that could be administered effi-ciently and from which one could generalize broad conclusions about students' science skills and knowledge? Zwick noted that a significant amount of research has shown that for real-world tasks, the level of difficulty a task represents tends to vary across test takers and to depend on the specific content of the task. In other words, there tend to be large task-by-person interactions. In a study that examined the California science test discussed above, for example, Shavelson and his colleagues (1993) found that nearly 50 percent of the variability in scores was attributable to such interactions (see also Baker et al., 1993; Stecher and Hamilton, 2009).

Yet another question is whether such tests can be equitable. As is the case with multiple-choice tests, Zwick noted, performance tests may inadvertently measure skills that are irrelevant to the construct—if some students are familiar with a topic and others are not, for example, or if a task requires students to write and writing skills are not the object of measurement. Limitations in mobil-ity and coordination may impede some students' access to hands-on experi-ments at stations or their capacity to manipulate the materials. Some students may have anxiety about responding to test items in a setting that is more public than individual paper-and-pencil testing. Almost any content and format could pose this sort of issue for some students, Zwick said, and research has shown that group differences are no less of a problem with performance assessment than they have been with multiple-choice assessment (see, e.g., Dunbar et al., 1991; Linn et al., 1991; Bond, 1995).

Reliability is generally lower for performance items scored by human raters than for multiple-choice items (see Lukhele et al., 1994). Achieving acceptable reliability rates may require extensive (and expensive) efforts for each task, including development and refinement of rubrics and training of raters. Zwick noted a number of challenges in trying to develop assessments that provide results that are comparable across years and from state to state. Performance tasks tend to be longer and more memorable than shorter ones, so security concerns would dictate that they not be repeated making linking difficult (as discussed below). Because performance tasks are more time consuming, students will generally complete fewer of them, another reason why reliability can be low and linkages difficult to establish.

Zwick also addressed some of the challenges of using computerized adaptive tests. She acknowledged the many benefits others had already identified, such as flexible administration, instant reporting, and more precise estimates of proficiency. However, she noted, development of these test requires significant resources. Very large numbers of items are needed—for example, the Graduate Management Admissions Test (GMAT) had a pool of 9,000 items when it converted to this format in 1997 and has steadily increased its pool since then (Rudner, 2010). A large pool of items is needed to cover a range of difficulty levels. Security is another concern, particularly in the case of high-stakes exams, such as the GMAT and Graduate Record Examination (GRE), where there is ample motivation for people to memorize items for use in test preparation. Thus, most programs use both multiple rotating pools of items and algorithms that control test takers' exposure to particular items.

With these concerns in mind, Zwick offered several recommendations. Psychometrics should be an integral part of the planning from the inception of a program, she said. That is, effective scoring and linking plans cannot be developed after data have been collected. Pilot testing of every aspect of an assessment is also very important, including test administration, human and machine scoring, and score reporting. And finally, she highlighted the importance of taking advantage of the lessons others have already learned, closing with a quotation from a 1994 paper on the Vermont Portfolio Assessment: "The basic lesson . . . is the need for modest expectations, patience, and ongoing evaluation in our national experimentation with innovative large-scale . . . assessments as a tool of educational reform" (Koretz et al., 1994).

CROSS-STATE COMPARISONS

One important reason to have common standards would be to establish common learning objectives for students regardless of where they live. But unless all students are also assessed with exactly the same instruments, comparing their learning across states is not so easily accomplished. Nevertheless, the capacity to make cross-state comparisons remains important to policy makers and educators. Ron Hambleton described some of the complex technical issues that surround this challenge, known to psychometricians as "linking": placing test results on the same score scale so that they can be compared.[2]

The basic issue that linking procedures are designed to address is the need to determine, when results from two tests appear to be different, whether that difference means that one of the tests is easier than the other or that one of the groups of students is more able than the other. There are several different statistical procedures for linking the results of different tests (see National Research Council, 1999a, 1999b).[3] If the tests were developed to measure precisely the same constructs, to meet the same specifications, and to produce scores on the same scale, the procedures are relatively straightforward. They are still very important though, since users count on the results of, say, the SAT (formerly, the Scholastic Aptitude Test), to mean exactly the same thing, year after year. More complex approaches are necessary when the tests are developed to different frameworks and specifications or yield scores on different scales. A common analogy is the formula for linking temperatures measured in degrees Fahrenheit or Celsius, but because of the complexity of the cognitive activities measured by educational tests, procedures for linking test scores are significantly more complex.

In general, Hambleton explained, in order to compare the achievement of different groups of students it is necessary to have some comparability not only in the standards that guide the assessment, but also in the tests and the curricula to which the students have been exposed. While much is in flux at the moment, Hambleton suggested that it appears likely that states will continue to use a variety of approaches to assessment, including combinations of paper-and-pencil format, computer-based assessment, and various kinds of innovative assessments. This multifaceted approach may be an effective way to support instruction at the state and district levels, he pointed out, but it will complicate tremendously the task of producing results that can be compared across states. Innovative item types are generally designed to measure new kinds of skills, but the more detailed and numerous the constructs measured become, the greater the challenge of linking the results of one assessment to those of another.

To demonstrate the challenge, Hambleton began with an overview of the complexity of linking traditional assessments. Even in the most strictly stan-

---

[2]Hambleton credited two reports from the National Research Council (1999a, 1999b) for much of his discussion.

[3]See also information from the National Center for Education Statistics, see http://nces.ed.gov/pubs98/linking/c3.asp [accessed August 2010]).

dardized testing program, it is nearly impossible to produce tests from year to year that are so clearly equivalent that scores can be compared without using statistical linking procedures. Even for the SAT, possibly the most thoroughly researched and well funded testing program in the world, psychometricians have not been able to get around the need to make statistical adjustments in order to link every different form of the test every year. There are two basic procedures involved in linking two test forms: first, to make sure either that some number of people take both test forms or that some number of items appear in both test forms, and, second, to use statistical procedures to adjust (in one of several ways) for any differences in difficulty between the two test forms that become apparent (see Hambleton, 2009).

The same must also be done if comparisons are to be made across states, Hambleton noted. This is easiest if the states share the same content standards and proficiency standards and also administer the same tests, as is the case with the New England Common Assessment Program (NECAP). However, even when these three elements are the same, it is still possible that items will perform differently across states because of variations in teaching methods, curricula, or other factors, and this possibility must be checked. Any changes to the nature or administration of a test may affect the way items perform. Thus, the addition of new item types, separate sections to measure an individual state's desired content, changes in the positioning of items, or conversion of certain parts of an assessment to computer delivery, may affect equating (see National Research Council, 1999a, 1999b). The timing of the test is also important: even if states have similar curricula, if they administer a common test at different points in the year it will affect the quality of the linking.

In addition, Hambleton noted, since common items are necessary to perform cross-state linking procedures, some of each type must be given to each group of test takers, and therefore scoring of constructed-response items must be precisely consistent across states. The testing conditions must be as close to identical as possible, including such operational features as test instructions, timing, and test security procedures, as well as larger issues, such as the stakes attached to test results. Even minor differences in answer sheet design or test book layout have the potential to interfere with item functioning (see National Research Council, 1999a, 1999b).

Computer-based testing adds to the complexity by potentially allowing administrations to vary in new ways (in time, in context, etc.) and also by requiring that all items be linked in advance. States and districts are likely to use different operating systems and platforms, which may affect seemingly minor details in the way tests look to students and the way they interact with them (e.g., how students scroll through the test or show their work), and these differences would have to be accounted for in the linking procedures. If there are not enough computers for every student to take an assessment at the same time, the testing window is usually extended, but doing that may affect both the linking and security.

Hambleton stressed that all of these constraints apply whether the desired comparison is between just two test forms or state assessments or among a number of states in a consortium that use the same assessment. If the comparison is extended across consortia, more significant sources of variation come into play, including multiple different sets of curricula, test design, performance standards, and so forth.

The essential principle of linking, for which Hambleton credited psychometrician Albert Beaton, is "if you want to measure change or growth over time don't change the measure." But this approach is completely impractical in the current context of educational testing, where change—in the content to be tested and in test design—is almost constant.

Moreover, Hambleton noted, most linking procedures rest on the idea that a test is unidimensional (i.e., that it measures skills in a single domain), but new forms of testing are multidimensional (they measure skills in more than one domain). So not only would linking have to account for each of the dimensions assessed, it would have to account for changing combinations of dimensions as tests evolve. Hambleton suggested that, at least in assessments used for summative purposes, it would be necessary to place some constraints on these factors to make linking possible.

Hambleton suggested that states' capacity to maintain high-quality linking procedures is already being stretched. With new sorts of assessments it will be critical to take seriously the need to expend resources to sustain the psychometric features that are needed to answer the questions policy makers ask. New research on questions about vertical scaling and linking tests that use multiple assessment modes, for example, will be necessary to support the current goals for assessment reform. A related, but equally important challenge will be that of displaying and reporting new kinds of data in ways that users can easily understand and report. The number of issues that are involved will ensure, Hambleton joked, that "no psychometrician will be left behind." He acknowledged, however, that they "can't just sit in their ivory towers and take 5 years to solve a problem."

PERSPECTIVES: PAST AND FUTURE

The importance of comparisons across states is seldom questioned now, but Zwick pointed out that this was not always the case. When the National Assessment of Educational Progress (NAEP) was first developed in the 1960s, she reminded participants, it was not designed to support such comparisons (Zwick, 2009). At that time, the public was very wary of federal involvement in education. Federal enforcement of school desegregation and the passage of the Civil Rights Act of 1964 and the Elementary and Secondary Education Act in 1965 were viewed as the limits of federal involvement in education that the public would accept, and state-by-state comparisons were viewed as potentially polarizing.

By the 1980s, however, the idea of promoting academic excellence through competition was becoming increasingly popular. President Ronald Reagan's 1984 State of the Union address called for comparisons of academic achievement among states and schools, arguing that "without standards and competition there can be no champions, no records broken, no excellence. . ." (Zwick, 2009). In response, the U.S. Department of Education first developed "wall charts," which displayed comparisons of the resources states committed to education and measures of performance, such as average SAT and ACT (American College Test) scores. These comparisons were widely viewed as un-illuminating at best, since the college admissions tests reflected only the performance of college-bound students and were not aligned to curriculum and instruction in the states. By the late 1980s, NAEP had developed its Trial State Assessment, which compared the mathematics performance of 8th graders in 37 states. By the mid-1990s, the state assessments were fully operational. Later in the decade, the Clinton administration proposed a "voluntary national test" as a way of collecting comparative information on individual students, but it was never implemented.

The NAEP state assessments received an additional boost when the No Child Left Behind (NCLB) Act made states' participation a condition for the receipt of Title I funding, Zwick noted. (Participation in NAEP is technically voluntary, and the program has in the past occasionally struggled to secure adequate representation for its matrix-sampling design.) NCLB also required states to meet various requirements for their own assessments and accountability provisions. Comparisons began to be made among states on the basis of the results of their own assessments, even though the assessments used different designs, proficiency standards, and so on. Studies of states' results have shown that states' definitions of proficiency vary significantly and tend to be lower than those used in NAEP (see National Research Council, 2008). This variation has contributed to the growing enthusiasm for common core standards.

The common core standards are likely to help states achieve economies of scale, as will their decisions to form consortia as part of the Race the Top competition, Laurie Wise noted. With more money to spend on assessment, states should be able to produce tests that are better aligned to standards, contain richer and more innovative items, and are more reliable. Results are likely to be reported more quickly and provide more useful information for diagnosing individual students' needs and guiding instruction. And states could more easily take advantage of a growing body of knowledge and experience as they collaborate to develop new approaches. Funding for research to improve cognitive analyses of test content, validity, and a many other issues could feed the development of more innovative assessments that are also feasible and affordable. The NECAP example has suggested to some that when standards and assessments are shared, states may be somewhat shielded from public reaction to disappointing results and correspondingly less likely to lower their performance standards to achieve nominally better results.

However, Hambleton made clear that there are significant challenges to making sure that state-to-state comparisons are valid, fair, and useful. One premise of the common core standards is that they will allow states to measure their students against the same expectations, but the rules permit states to supplement the core standards with up to 15 percent of additional content they value. To illustrate, Zwick suggested quantifying the standards and assuming that the 10 states in a consortium share 85 standards, and that each has its own 15 additional unique standards. In that case, of the total of $85 + 10(15) = 235$ standards, only $85/235(100)$, or 36.2 percent, would be shared among the 10 states. Since no single assessment is likely to cover all of a state's standards, the content shared by each of the 10 state assessments could be significantly lower.

Hambleton reiterated that every source of variation among state tests can impair the ability to produce comparable results and report them on the same scale. Moreover, he noted, curriculum and instruction will not be shared, even if states share standards. States are likely to find it very difficult to adhere to common procedures for every aspect of testing (preparation, administration, booklet or format design, accommodations, etc.). States also differ in terms of demographic characteristics, per-pupil expenditures, teacher training, class size, and many other features that are likely to affect test results.

Zwick had several suggestions for states to support meaningful comparison across the states:

- Provide as much context as possible: Document differences across states in order to provide a context for comparisons.
- Make the test instrument and testing policies as similar as possible: Collaborate on scoring and reporting methods and make sure that format, instructions, and protocols for each phase of assessment (including preparation) are uniform. Put unique state items in a separate section to minimize their influence on students' performance of the common items. Develop an adequate pool of items in each area of interest.
- Invest in research and professional development: provide training to school administrators and teachers in the interpretation and uses of test scores.

Zwick also advocated fostering collaboration among psychometricians, educators, and policy makers, who, despite their differences in perspective, are likely to be pursuing the same goal—the improvement of teaching and learning in U.S. classrooms.

Some participants suggested that many of the problems with state comparisons could be solved if states opted to use common assessments, but others responded that the many sources of variation among states still remain. Several commented that other countries have had success with common curricula and common tests, and for some that seems like the best route. Others pointed out that NAEP already provides state comparisons, though without any particular alignment to the standards to which states are working and without scores for individual students.

9

Research Needs

There is wide public acceptance of the value of a system in which assessments measure student progress in meeting education standards and the test results are used to hold students, schools, educators, and jurisdictions to account for their performance. But, Lorrie Shepard pointed out in the summary session, two very different theories of action regarding the way such a system will actually bring about improvements have been put forward. And neither the differences between them nor the implications of adopting one or the other have been widely recognized.

THEORY AND GOALS

The incentives theory, as she called the first approach, is that given sufficient motivation, teachers and other school personnel will develop ways to improve instruction. This perspective was the basis for the Elementary and Secondary Education Act of 1994, which required states to establish standards and assessments. The other approach, which Shepard called the coherent capacity-building theory, posited that an additional step—beyond establishing clear expectations and the motivation to meet them—was needed. Educators would also need the capacity, in the form of professional development and other supports, to improve their teaching in order for the accountability measures to have the desired effect (see, e.g., National Research Council, 1995). Shepard suggested that the incentives theory is dominant, and that capacity building has been neglected.

Similar imprecision is evident in the possible interpretations of some of the top reform goals of the present moment, Shepard suggested, including:

- reforming assessments using conceptually rich tasks,
- integrating 21st-century skills and academic content,
- creating coherence between large-scale and classroom assessments, and
- using data to improve classroom instruction.

For example, treating the first two bullets as distinct enterprises makes little sense, given that the research on the developmental nature of learning seems to suggest the importance of weaving content and higher-order thinking skills together (see Chapter 2).

Shepard said she believes that policy makers do not completely understand that effective teaching relies on a model for how learning proceeds, in which cognitive skills and the knowledge of when and how to use them develop together with content knowledge and understanding of how to generalize from it. She suggested that, without this theory of learning, policy makers are likely to accept current modes of assessment. They may believe, for example, that narrowing the curriculum is necessary because basic reading and mathematics skills are so important. They may not be aware that excessive drill on work-sheets that resemble summative tests does not give students the opportunity to understand the context and purpose for what they are learning—which would enhance their skill development (see Elmore, 2003; Blanc et al., 2010; Bulkley et al., 2010; Olah et al., 2010). Similarly, although policy makers are in favor of data-driven decision making, Shepard said, she believes that many educators lack the substantive expertise to interpret the available data and use it to make meaningful changes in their practice.

During the workshop discussions, many presenters drew attention to the churning that affects education policy because of shifts in political goals and personnel at the state level. Given that reality, coherence will have to come at a lower level, Shepard argued. The United States does not have a common curriculum, she suggested, because it has no tradition of relying on subject matter experts in many decisions about education. Psychometricians and policy makers have typically taken the lead in the development of assessments, for example: subject matter experts have generally been involved in some way, but they are not usually asked to oversee the development of frameworks, item development, and the interpretation of results.

Now, however, the interests of subject-matter experts and cognitive researchers who have been developing models of student learning within particular disciplines have converged, and this convergence offers the possibility of a coherence that could withstand the inevitable fluctuations in political interests. However, the practical application of this way of thinking about learning is not yet widely understood, Shepard observed. Thus, for Shepard, the opportunity of the present moment is to take the first steps in inventing and implementing the necessary innovations. It is not practical to expect that any one state or consortium could develop an ideal system for all grades and subject areas on the first try, so the focus should be on incremental improvements. She suggested that each consortium grant award should be focused on the development of a system of "next-generation, high-quality" classroom and summative assessments for one manageable area—say, for mathematics for grades 4 through 8.

She noted that Lauren Resnick has proposed a way of implementing innovative approaches incrementally. Resnick has suggested that content-based "modules" that incorporate both a rich curriculum and associated assessments could be adopted one by one and incrementally incorporated into an existing full curriculum. In the near term, this would leave existing assessments unchanged, but, over time, the accumulating body of new modules would eventually lead to a completely transformed system, in which accountability information could be drawn from the assessment components of the innovative curriculum modules. This approach would allow educators to proceed gradually, as the research to support the development of such modules grows, and also to sidestep many of the political and practical challenges that have hampered past programs.

Shepard also emphasized the importance of considering curriculum along with new and improved assessment models. She cautioned that establishing higher standards means not only setting cut-points at a higher level than they are currently, but also incorporating material of a substantively different character into assessments. If this is done without corresponding changes to curriculum and instruction, the result will be predictable—students are likely not to succeed on the new assessment. In the end, after all, the purpose of the improvements, she said, is to "change the character of what we teach and then make those opportunities available to all students and make sure that the assessment can track any changes over time."

Shepard closed by reminding everyone that "to truly transform learning opportunities in classrooms in ways that research indicates are possible, it will be necessary to remove [existing impediments], especially low-level tests that misdirect effort; provide coherent curricula consistent with ambitious reforms; and take seriously the need for capacity-building at every level of the education system."

In Diana Pullin's summary remarks, she also focused on the opportunity presented not only by the Race to the Top funds, but also by what appears to be an important evolution in the thinking of many policy makers and educators about the purposes and potential of assessment. The federal funding, she observed, has presented an opportunity, but, "we are on a fragile edge [between] being able to do something new and better and dramatically differ-ent, or something that is only a slight improvement or perhaps a step back."

A number of challenges complicate the picture, she said. Limitations in teacher preparation and in-service development have left teachers not yet ready to interpret and use the kind of rich information hoped for from innovative assessments. The capacity of the testing industry to keep pace with a rapid shift in priorities for state testing is not clear. The workshop discussions did not offer any formulas for the necessary innovation, she noted, but innovation by definition cannot be accomplished by formula. Pullin said the real challenge may be to push past the boundaries that may have confined people's thinking. Those in the assessment community may not have the knowledge and skills about leaning theory and the education of students with disabilities or English language learners, and those in the discipline and curriculum communities may not have thorough understanding of assessment. Yet these intellectual traditions and perspectives must be integrated if a new generation of assessments is to be successful.

Others shared the concern that there is risk in the current situation. Discussant Joe Willhoft noted that there is little doubt that assessments influ-ence instruction and learning—and that existing ones can do so to good effect. For example, he said, he believes that a writing assessment used in Washington state yielded significant changes in instruction and in expectations, and, in turn, marked improvements in students' writing skills. His concern is that many questions about how new, consortium-based assessment systems might work have yet to be answered.

Discussant Deborah Seligman addressed a similar theme. She noted that the education community appears to be ready for a change in thinking about assessments, but that states' economies may not be robust enough to sustain the full-bore effort necessary for it to be a success. She noted that even though most educators and policy makers would agree that writing is one of the most important domains to assess, California cut this assessment first: it did so not for substantive reasons but because the program is expensive and easy to separate form other elements of the assessment program. Politics, she observed, is either the factor that can make things happen or the largest obstacle to progress.

Nevertheless, Gene Wilhoit commented, there is a general political con-sensus to move rapidly in this new direction. The common core standards are laying the groundwork for this change, but the policy decisions that will follow—and need to be made quite rapidly—will have a profound impact on public education for the next generation. He said that those making these deci-sions should be urged to pay close attention to the guidance of experts and the examples of countries that are far ahead of the United States as they proceed. Many others agreed, and a representative final word of caution might be, in the words of Rebecca Zwick, "don't put all your eggs in that basket. Have a plan B.

Have something else you know you can score and report, but at the same time have a piece that you are using to explore innovative ideas."

RESEARCH PRIORITIES

Shepard and other discussants were asked to reflect on their highest priorities for research that would support progress in developing and implementing innovative assessments. Many of the ideas overlapped, and they fell into a few categories: measurement; content; teaching and learning, and experimentation.

Measurement Many participants emphasized the need for psychometric models that were developed generations ago to be updated in light of recent research on learning and cognition. New ways of thinking about what should be measured and what sort of information would be useful to educators have been put forward (see Chapter 2), and it is clear that current psychometric models do not fit them well. The new models illustrate, for example, the importance of each of the stages that students go through in learning complex material. This idea implies that teachers (and students) need information about students' developing understanding of concepts and facts and how they fit into a larger intellectual structure. Yet educational measurement has tended to focus on one-dimensional rankings according to students' mastery of specific knowledge and skills at a given time. The goals of traditional psychometrics remain important, but perhaps need to be stretched. Means of establishing the validity of new kinds of assessments for new kinds of uses are needed.

Discussants pointed to the need for a strategy for making sure that the information an assessment provides is being used to good effect and a strategy for checking the links in a proposed learning trajectory, to be sure each stage in the progression is reasonable and well supported. The capacity to compare results across assessments is already being stretched, and the introduction of more innovative modes of assessment may present challenges that cannot be solved with current procedures. But the policy demand for comparative information suggests a need for new thinking about the precise questions that are important and the kinds of information that can provide satisfactory answers.

Other fields, one participant noted, have grappled with similar issues. In medicine, for example, simulations are used in credentialing assessments, despite the lack of procedures for equating precisely across assessments that use simulations. It would be worthwhile to explore the decisions that the medical profession made and their outcomes. It may be, for example, that the technical standards for modes of assessment could vary somewhat, according to the intended purpose to which the results will be put.

A final thought offered on measurement was that the measurement community should be conducting basic research that addresses not only immediate problems, but also the challenges and technological changes that are likely to emerge a decade from now. Some participants responded that the capacity of the testing profession is already being stretched and that there is little leisure for this kind of thinking—while others stressed the importance of looking ahead.

Content The measurement community may need to catch up with advances in cognitive research, but the overall picture of what students should learn is perhaps even less complete, Mark Wilson and others noted. Deeper cognitive analysis of the content to be taught and assessed is still needed. Detailed learning trajectories have been put forward in a few areas of science and mathematics, but they are only a beginning. Understanding of the barriers to advancing along a trajectory, and of the efficacy of different approaches to teaching students to overcome those barriers, are in the beginning stages. Outside of science and mathematics, even less progress has been made in tracing learning trajectories.

Without a much broader base of research on these questions, the progress in developing innovative assessments will be hampered. Policy makers are currently working from hypothesized trajectories of how learning in reading, English/language arts, and mathematics progresses from kindergarten through grade 12. These need to be elaborated, and the field needs a plan for gathering data about the validity of the common core standards that are based on them and for improving the descriptions of the trajectories.

Teaching and Learning An important theme of the workshop was the intimate relationship between models of measurement and models of teaching and learning. If assessments are to play the valuable role in education that many envision, they must not only align with what is known about how students think and learn, but also provide meaningful information that educators can use. As many speakers emphasized, if educators are to play their part, their preparation and professional development must encompass this new thinking about assessment and the means to use it. Research is needed to support these changes. Teachers also have much to contribute to evolving thinking about teaching and assessment. Involving them in the research will be critical to ensuring that new kinds of assessment data can really improve instruction.

It is not only data that teachers need, though, some participants pointed out. Their capacity to reflect on and evaluate not only their own practice and capacity to adapt, but also the value of innovations they are asked to try, is also important. Working individually, in small groups, as whole departments, or even as schools, they can provide a check on such questions as the practical application of theoretical learning trajectories.

Experimentation Rebecca Zwick and others noted that there is no one optimal assessment system waiting to be discovered. A range of international models offer promising possibilities and should be explored in greater detail. The development of state consortia offers the opportunity for the education community to explore a variety of different models and the theories that underlie them and to work out a variety of ways of addressing key system goals. The idea that educators and policy makers should experiment on students may have negative connotations, but many participants also spoke about the critical importance of taking innovation step by step and learning from each step. In no other field, one participant pointed out, would policy makers overlook the importance of research and development to something as important as redesigning the assessment system. Ideally, the process would begin with a clear picture of the questions that need answers and the development of a strategy for researching those questions and testing hypotheses.

Several participants noted that state consortia, individual states, districts, schools, teachers, and students can all contribute to the design of new aspects of assessment systems and the important work of trying them out and collecting information about what works well and what does not. More typical, however, has been a model in which a whole new assessment system is created and presented to the public as ready to be implemented statewide. The big risk in such an approach is that implementation problems could doom an idea with valuable potential before it had a chance to be fully implemented or that individual valuable features of the approach would be thrown out along with features that did not work.

Echoing the comments of Lorrie Shepard, several participants suggested that retaining some or all of the elements of existing assessment systems, while gradually incorporating new elements, would allow for both the development of political and public acceptance and the flexibility to benefit from experience. An incremental approach may also make it possible to address different aspects of a system in a way that would be too radical to attempt for the whole. Whether the innovations are new instructional units based on common core standards, in which assessment is embedded; revised curricula that better map the learning trajectories in new standards; or new formats and designs for summative assessments; or some other innovation, it should be possible to gradually construct a coherent system that meets the needs for both accountability and instructional guidance.

References

Alpert, T., and Slater, S. (2010). *A Coherent Approach to Adaptive Assessment.* Presentation prepared for the workshop of the Committee on Best Practices in State Assessment Systems: Improving Assessment while Revisiting Standards, National Research Council, Washington, DC, April 6-7, 2010. Available: http://www7.nationalacademies.org/bota/Best_Practices_for_State_Assessment_presentation_Alpert.pdf [accessed September 2010].

American Educational Research Association, American Psychological Association, and National Council on Measurement in Education Joint Committee on Standards for Educational and Psychological Testing. (1999). *Standards for Educational and Psychological Testing.* Washington, DC: American Educational Research Association.

Baker, E.L., O'Neil, H.F., and Linn, R.L. (1993). Policy and validity prospects for performance-based assessment. *American Psychologist, 48,* 1,210-1,218.

Bennett, R. (2010). *Innovative Assessment Systems: The Role of New Technology.* Presentation prepared for the workshop of the Committee on Best Practices in State Assessment Systems: Improving Assessment while Revisiting Standards, National Research Council, Washington, DC, April 6-7, 2010. Available: http://www7.nationalacademies.org/bota/Best_Practices_for_State_Assessment_presentation_Bennett.pdf [accessed September 2010].

Bishop, J. (1997). *The Effect of Curriculum-Based Exit Exam Systems on Student Achievement* (Working paper no. 97-15). Ithaca, NY: Center for Advanced Human Resource Studies, Cornell University. Abstract Available: http://digitalcommons.ilr.cornell.edu/cahrswp/156/ [accessed September 2010].

Blanc, S., Christman, J.B., Liu, R., Mitchell, C., Travers, E., and Bulkley, K.E. (2010). Learning to learn from data: Benchmarks and instructional communities. *Peabody Journal of Education, 85*(2), 205-225.

Bond, L. (1995). Unintended consequences of performance assessment: Issues of bias and fairness. *Educational Measurement: Issues and Practice, 14,* 21-24.

Bulkley, K., Christman, J., Goertz, M., and Lawrence, N. (2010). Building with benchmarks: The role of the district in Philadelphia's benchmark assessment system. *PJE. Peabody Journal of Education, 85*(2), 186-204. Abstract available: http://www.informaworld.com/smpp/content~db=all~content=a921425767 [accessed September 2010].

Cagle, P. (2010). *How Assessments Could Inform Instruction.* Presentation Prepared for the workshop of the Committee on Best Practices for State Assessment Systems: Improving Assessment While Revisiting Standards, National Research Council, Washington, DC, April 6-7, 2010. Available: http://www7.nationalacademies.org/bota/Best_Practices_for_State_Assessment_presentation_Cagle.pdf [accessed September 2010].

Christman, J., Neild, R., Bulkley, K., Blanc, S., Liu, R., Mitchell, C., and Travers, E. (2009). *Making the Most of Interim Assessment Data. Lessons from Philadelphia.* Philadelphia, PA: Research for Action.

Chudowsky, N., and Chudowsky, V. (2007). *No Child Left Behind at Five: A Review of Changes to State Accountability Plans.* Washington, DC: Center on Education Policy.

Clune, W.H., and White, P.A. (2008). *Policy Effectiveness of Interim Assessments in Providence Public Schools.* (WCER Working Paper No. 2008-10, Wisconsin Center for Education Research.) Madison: University of Wisconsin.

Cook, H.G. (in press). *FLARE Language Learning Targets.* Madison: Wisconsin Center for Education Research.

Cortiella, C., and Burnette, J. (2008). *Challenging Change: How schools and Districts Are Improving the Performance of Special Education Students.* New York: National Center for Learning Disabilities. Available: http://www.ncld.org/images/stories/OnCapitolHill/PolicyRelatedPublications/ChallengingChange/ChallengingChange.pdf [accessed September 2010].

Cronin, J., Dahlin, M. Xiang, Y., and McCahon, D. (2009). *The Accountability Illusion.* Washington, DC: Thomas B. Fordham Institute. Available: http://www.evsd.org/documents/accountability.pdf [accessed September 2010].

Darling-Hammond, L. (2010). *Curriculum-Embedded Performance Assessments.* Presentation Prepared for the workshop of the Committee on Best Practices for State Assessment Systems: Improving Assessment While Revisiting Standards, National Research Council, Washington, DC, April 6-7, 2010. Available: http://www7.nationalacademies.org/bota/Best_Practices_for_State_Assessment_presentation_Darling-Hammond1.pdf [accessed September 2010].

Dunbar, S.B, Koretz, D.M., and Hoover, H.D. (1991). Quality control in the development and use of performance assessments. *Applied Measurement in Education, 4,* 289-303.

Elmore, R.F. (2003). Accountability and capacity. In M. Carnoy, R.F. Elmore, and L.S. Siskin (Eds.), *High Schools and the New Accountability* (pp. 195-209). New York: Routledge.

Ferrara, S. (2009). *The Maryland School Performance Assessment Program (MSPAP) 1991-2002: Political Considerations.* Paper prepared for the workshop of the Committee on Best Practices in State Assessment Systems: Improving Assessment while Revisiting Standards, National Research Council, Washington, DC, December 10-11, 2009. Available: http://www7.nationalacademies.org/bota/Steve%20Ferrara.pdf [accessed September 2010].

Fuchs, T., and Woessmann, L. (2007). What accounts for international differences in student performance? A re-examination using the PISA data. *Empirical Economics, 32*(2-3), 433-464.

Fuller, B., Gesicki, K., Kang, E., and Wright, J. (2006). *Is the No Child Left Behind Act Working? The Reliability of How States Track Achievement.* (Working Paper No.06-1). Berkeley: University of California and Stanford University, Policy Analysis for California Education.

Goertz, M.E. (2009). *Overview of Current Assessment Practices.* Paper prepared for the workshop of the Committee on Best Practices in State Assessment Systems: Improving Assessment while Revisiting Standards, National Research Council, Washington, DC, December 10-11, 2009. Available: http://www7.nationalacademies.org/bota/Peg_Goertz_Paper.pdf [accessed September 2010].

Goertz, M.E., Olah, L.N., and Riggan, M. (2009). *Can Interim Assessments Be Used for Instructional Change?* CPRE Policy Briefs: Reporting on Issues and Research in Education Policy and Finance. Available: http://www.cpre.org/images/stories/cpre_pdfs/rb_51_role%20policy%20brief_final%20web.pdf [accessed August 2010].

Gong, B. (2009). *Innovative Assessment in Kentucky's KIRIS System: Political Considerations.* Paper prepared for the workshop of the Committee on Best Practices in State Assessment Systems: Improving Assessment while Revisiting Standards, National Research Council, Washington, DC, December 10-11, 2009. Available: http://www7.nationalacademies.org/bota/Brian%20Gong.pdf [accessed September 2010].

Government Accounting Office. (2003). *Characteristics of Tests Will Influence Expenses; Information Sharing May Help States Realize Efficiencies.* GAO Report-03-389. Available: www.gao.gov/cgi-bin/getrpt?GAO-03-389 [accessed November 2009].

Government Accounting Office. (2009). *No Child Left Behind Act: Enhancements in the Department of Education's Review Process Could Improve State Academic Assessments.* GAO Report-09-911. Available: www.gao.gov/cgi-bin/getrpt?GAO-09-911 [accessed November 2009].

Hambleton, R.K. (2009). *Using Common Standards to Enable Cross-National Comparisons.* Paper prepared for the workshop of the Committee on Best Practices for State Assessment Systems: Improving Assessment While Revisiting Standards, National Research Council, Washington, DC, December 10-11. Available: http://www7.nationalacademies.org/bota/Ron_Hambleton.pdf [accessed September 2010].

Heritage, M. (2010). *Making Use of Assessment Information.* Presentation for the workshop of the Committee on Best Practices for State Assessment Systems: Improving Assessment While Revisiting Standards, National Research Council, Washington, DC, April 6-7, 2010. Available: http://www7.nationalacademies.org/bota/Best_Practices_for_State_Assessment_presentation_Heritage.pdf [accessed September 2010].

Heritage, M., Kim, J., Vendlinksi, T., and Herman, J. (2009). From evidence to action: A seamless process in formative assessment? *Educational Measurement: Issues and Practice, 28*(3), 24-31.

Herman, J. (2010). *Next Generation Assessment Systems: Toward Coherence and Utility.* Presentation for Workshop II of the Committee on Best Practices for State Assessment Systems: Improving Assessment While Revisiting Standards, National Research Council, Washington, DC, April 6-7, 2010. Available: http://www7.nationalacademies.org/bota/Best_Practices_for_State_Assessment_presentation_Herman.pdf [accessed September 2010].

Herman, J., Osmundson, E., and Silver, D. (2010). *Capturing Quality in Formative Assessment Practice: Measurement Challenges.* Los Angeles, CA: National Center for Research on Evaluation, Standards, and Student Testing and the University of California, Los Angeles. Available: http://www.cse.ucla.edu/products/reports/R770.pdf [accessed August 2010].

Hess, K. (2010). *Strategies for Helping Teachers Make Better Use of Assessment Results.* Presentation for Workshop II of the Committee on Best Practices for State Assessment Systems: Improving Assessment While Revisiting Standards, National Research Council, Washington, DC, April 6-7, 2010. Available: http://www7.nationalacademies.org/bota/Best_Practices_for_State_Assessment_presentation_Hess.pdf [accessed September 2010].

Hess, K., Kurizaki, V., and Holt, L. (2009). *Reflections on Tools and Strategies Used in the Hawaii Progress Maps Project: Lessons Learned from Learning Progressions.* Available: http://www.nciea.org/publications/Hawaii%20Lessons%20Learned_KH09.pdf [accessed September 2010].

Ho, A.D. (2008). The problem with "proficiency": Limitations of statistics and policy under No Child Left Behind. *Education Researcher, 37*(6), 351-360.

Jennings, J., and Rentner, D.S. (2006). Ten big effects of No Child Left Behind on public schools. *Phi Delta Kappan, 88*(2), 110-113.

Kirst, M., and J. Mazzeo (1996). The rise, fall, and rise of state assessment in California: 1993-1996. *Phi Delta Kappan, 78*(4), 319-323.

Koretz, D., and Barron, S. (1998). *The Validity of Gains on the Kentucky Instructional Results Information System (KIRIS).* Santa Monica, CA: RAND.

Koretz, D., Stecher, B., Klein, S., and McCaffrey, D. (1994). The Vermont portfolio assessment program: Findings and implications. *Educational Measurement: Issues and Practice, 13*(3), 5-16.

Koretz, D., Mitchell., K., Barron S., and Keith, S. (1996). *Perceived Effects of the Maryland School Performance Assessment Program*. Final Report, Project 3.2 State Accountability Models in Action. National Center for Research on Evaluation. Washington, DC: U.S. Department of Education.

Krajcik, J., McNeill, K.L., and Reiser, B., (2008). Learning-goals-driven design model: Developing curriculum materials that align with national standards and incorporate project-based pedagogy. *Science Education, 92*(1), 1-32.

Krajcik, J., Stevens, S., and Shin, N. (2009). *Developing Standards That Lead to Better Instruction and Learning*. Paper prepared for the workshop of the Committee on Best Practices for State Assessment Systems: Improving Assessment While Revisiting Standards, National Research Council, Washington, DC, December 10-11, 2009. Available: http://www7.nationalacademies. org/bota/Krajcik_Stevens_Paper.pdf [accessed September 2010].

Lai, E.R., and Waltman, K. (2008). *The Impact of NCLB on Instruction: A Comparison of Results for 2004-05 to 2006-07*. IARP Report #7. Iowa City: Center for Evaluation and Assessment, University of Iowa.

Lane, S., Ventrice, J., Cerrillo, T., Parke, C., and Stone, C. (1999). *Impact of the Maryland School Performance Assessment Program (MSPAP): Evidence from the Principal, Teacher, and Student Questionnaires (Reading, Writing, and Science)*. Paper presented at the Annual meeting of the National Council on Measurement in Education (Montreal, Quebec, Canada, April 19-23, 1999). Available: http://eric.ed.gov/PDFS/ED434928.pdf [accessed September 2010].

Lazer, S. (2009). *Technical Challenges with Innovative Item Types*. Paper prepared for the workshop of the Committee on Best Practices for State Assessment Systems: Improving Assessment While Revisiting Standards, National Research Council, Washington, DC, December 10-11, 2009. Available: http://www7.nationalacademies.org/bota/Steve%20Lazer.pdf [accessed September 2010].

Lindquist, E.F. (1951). Preliminary considerations in objective test construction. In E.F. Lindquist (Ed.), *Educational Measurement* (pp. 119-158). Washington, DC: American Council on Education.

Linn, R.L., Baker, E.L., and Dunbar, S.B. (1991). Complex, performance-based assessment: Expectations and validation criteria. *Educational Researcher, 20*, 15-21.

Linquanti, R. (2010). *Issues to Consider with Innovative Assessments: How Will English Language Learners Participate?* Presentation for Workshop II of the Committee on Best Practices for State Assessment Systems: Improving Assessment While Revisiting Standards, National Research Council, Washington, DC, April 6-7, 2010. Available: http://www7.nationalacademies.org/ bota/Best_Practices_for_State_Assessment_presentation_Linquanti.pdf [accessed September 2010].

Lukhele, R., Thissen, D., and Wainer, H. (1994). On the relative value of multiple-choice, constructed-response, and examinee-selected items on two achievement tests. *Journal of Educational Measurement, 31*, 234-250.

Marion, S. (2009). *Changes in Assessments and Assessment Systems Since 2002*. Paper prepared for the workshop of the Committee on Best Practices in State Assessment Systems: Improving Assessment while Revisiting Standards, National Research Council, Washington, DC, December 10-11. Available: http://www7.nationalacademies.org/bota/Scott%20Marion.pdf [accessed September 2010].

Mattson, D. (2009). *Science Assessment in Minnesota*. Paper prepared for the workshop of the Committee on Best Practices in State Assessment Systems: Improving Assessment while Revisiting Standards, National Research Council, Washington, DC, December 10-11. Available: http:// www7.nationalacademies.org/bota/Dirk_Mattson.pdf [accessed September 2010].

McMurrer, J. (2007). *Choices, Changes, and Challenges; Curriculum and Instruction in the NCLB Era*. Washington, DC: Center on Education Policy.

McTighe, J., and Wiggins, G. (1998). *Understanding by Design*. Alexandria, VA: Association for Supervision and Curriculum Development.

Mislevy, R. (1998). Foundations of a new test theory. In N. Fredericksen, R.J. Mislevy and I.I. Bejar (Eds.), *Test Theory for a New Generation of Tests* (pp. 19-38). Hillsdale, NJ: Erlbaum.

Mislevy, R.J., and Riconscente, M. (2005). *Evidence-Centered Assessment Design: Layers, Structures, and Terminology.* Menlo Park, CA: SRI International.

National Research Council. (1995). *Anticipating Goals 2000: Standards, Assessment, and Public Policy: Summary of a Workshop.* Board on Testing and Assessment, Center for Education. Washington, DC: National Academy Press.

National Research Council. (1996). *National Science Education Standards.* National Committee on Science Education Standards and Assessment. Washington DC: National Academy Press.

National Research Council. (1999a). *Embedding Questions: The Pursuit of a Common Measure in Uncommon Tests.* Committee on Embedding Common Test Items in State and District Assessments. D.M. Koretz, M.W. Bertenthal, and B.F. Green (Eds.). Division of Behavioral and Social Sciences and Education. Washington DC: National Academy Press.

National Research Council. (1999b). *Uncommon Measures: Equivalence and Linkage Among Educational Tests.* Committee on Equivalency and Linkage of Educational Tests. M.J. Feuer, P.W. Holland, B.F. Green, M.W. Bertenthal, and F.C. Hemphill (Eds.). Division of Behavioral and Social Sciences and Education. Washington, DC: National Academy Press.

National Research Council. (2001). *Knowing What Students Know.* Committee on the Foundations of Assessment. J. Pellegrino, N. Chudowsky, and R. Glaser (Eds). Board on Testing and Assessment. Washington, DC: National Academy Press.

National Research Council. (2005). *Systems for State Science Assessment.* Committee on Test Design for K-12 Science Achievement. M.R. Wilson and M.W. Bertenthal (Eds.). Center for Education, Division of Behavioral and Social Sciences and Education. Washington DC: The National Academies Press.

National Research Council. (2008). *Common Standards for K-12 Education? Considering the Evidence: Summary of a Workshop Series.* A. Beatty, Rapporteur. Committee on State Standards in Education: A Workshop Series. Center for Education, Division of Behavioral and Social Sciences and Education. Washington, DC: The National Academies Press.

Olah, L., Lawrence, N., and Riggan, M. (2010). Learning to learn from benchmark assessment data: How teachers analyze results. *Peabody Journal of Education, 85*(2), 226-245.

Perie, M., Marion, S., and Gong, B. (2007). *The Role of Interim Assessments in a Comprehensive Assessment System: A Policy Brief.* Center for Assessment, The Aspen Institute, and Achieve, Inc. Available: http://www.achieve.org/files/TheRoleofInterimAssessments.pdf [accessed March 2010].

Porter, A.C., Polikoff, M.S., and Smithson, J. (2009). Is there a de facto national intended curriculum? Evidence from state content standards. *Educational Evaluation and Policy Analysis, 31*(3), 238-268.

Roeber, E. (2010). *Designing High Quality, Affordable Assessment Systems.* Presentation for Workshop II of the Committee on Best Practices for State Assessment Systems: Improving Assessment While Revisiting Standards, National Research Council, Washington, DC, April 6-7, 2010. Available: http://www7.nationalacademies.org/bota/Best_Practices_for_State_Assessment_presentation_Roeber.pdf [accessed September 2010].

Rudner, L. (2010). Implementing the GMAT computerized adaptive test. In W. Van der Linden and C.A.W. Glas (Eds.), *Elements of Adaptive Testing* (pp. 151-166). Available: http://www.springerlink.com/content/k221l4l4r64x7316/fulltext.pdf [accessed September 2010].

Schmidt, W.H., Wang, H.C., and McKnight, C. (2005). Curriculum coherence: An examination of U.S. mathematics and science content standards from an international perspective. *Journal of Curriculum Studies, 37,* 525-559.

Shavelson, R.J., Baxter, G.P., and Gao, X. (1993). Sampling variability of science assessments. *Journal of Educational Measurement, 30,* 215-232.

Shepard, L. (1993). Evaluating test validity. *Review of Research in Education, 19*(1), 405-450.

Shin, N., Stevens, S., and Krajcik, J. (in press) *Using Construct-Centered Design as a Systematic Approach for Tracking Student Learning Over Time.* London, England: Routledge, Taylor & Francis Group.

Smith, C.L., Wiser, M., Anderson, C.W., and Krajcik, J. (2006) Implications of research on children's learning for standards and assessment: A proposed learning progression for matter and the atomic-molecular theory. *Measurement: Interdisciplinary Research and Perspectives,* 4(1), 1-98.

Smith, M., and O'Day, J. (1991). Systematic school reform. In S. Fuhrman and B. Malen (Eds.),*The Politics of Curriculum and Testing* (pp. 233-267). Philadelphia: Falmer Press.

Stecher, B., and Hamilton, L. (2009). *What Have We Learned from Pioneers in Innovative Assessment?* Paper prepared for the workshop of the Committee on Best Practices for State Assessment Systems: Improving Assessment While Revisiting Standards, National Research Council, Washington, DC, December 10-11, 2009. Available: http://www7.nationalacademies. org/bota/Brian_Stecher_and_Laura_Hamilton.pdf [accessed September 2010].

Stecher, B.M., Epstein, S., Hamilton, L.S., Marsh, J.A., Robyn, A., McCombs, J.S., Russell, J.L., and Naftel, S. (2008). *Pain and Gain: Implementing No Child Left Behind in California, Georgia, and Pennsylvania, 2004 to 2006.* Santa Monica, CA: RAND.

Stevens, S., Sutherland, L., and Krajcik, J.S. (2009). *The Big Ideas of Nanoscale Science and Engineering.* Arlington, VA: National Science Teachers Association Press.

Sunderman, G.L., Ed. (2008). *Holding NCLB Accountable: Achieving Accountability, Equity, and School Reform.* Thousand Oaks, CA: Corwin Press.

Thurlow, M. (2010). *Issues to Consider with Innovative Assessments: Students with Disabilities Perspectives.* Presentation for Workshop II of the Committee on Best Practices for State Assessment Systems: Improving Assessment While Revisiting Standards, National Research Council, Washington, DC, April 6-7, 2010. Available: http://www7.nationalacademies.org/ bota/Best_Practices_for_State_Assessment_presentation_Thurlow.pdf [accessed September 2010].

Toch, T. (2006). *Margins of Error: The Education Testing Industry in the No Child Left Behind Era.* Washington, DC: Education Sector.

Topol, B., Olsen, J., and Roeber, E. (2010). *The Cost of New High-Quality Assessments: A Comprehensive Analysis of the Potential Costs for Future State Assessments.* Stanford, CA: Stanford Center for Opportunity Policy in Education.

Tucker, M. (2010). *BOTA Workshop on Best Practices for State Assessment.* Presentation prepared for Workshop II of the Committee on Best Practices for State Assessment Systems: Improving Assessment While Revisiting Standards, National Research Council, Washington, DC, April 6-7, 2010. Available: http://www7.nationalacademies.org/bota/Best_Practices_for_ State_Assessment_presentation_Tucker.pdf [accessed September 2010].

U.S. Department of Education. (2009). *Race to the Top Program Executive Summary* Available: http://www.ed.gov/programs/racetothetop/resources.html [accessed January 2010].

Wilde, J. (2010). *Comparing Results of the NAEP Long-Term Trend Assessment: ELLs, Former ELLs, and English-Proficient Students.* Paper presented at the 2010 American Educational Research Association Annual meeting. Washington, DC: American Educational Research Association. Available: http://www.ncela.gwu.edu/files/uploads/16/AERA_2010_Wilde.pdf [accessed September 2010].

Wilson, M., Ed. (2004). *Towards Coherence Between Classroom Assessment and Accountability. 103rd Yearbook of the National Society for the Study of Education, Part II.* Chicago, IL: The University of Chicago Press.

Wilson, M. (2005). *Constructing Measures: An Item-Response Modeling Approach.* Mahwah, NJ: Erlbaum.

Wilson, M. (2009). *Developing Assessment Tasks That Lead to Better Instruction and Learning.* Paper prepared for the workshop of the Committee on Best Practices for State Assessment Systems: Improving Assessment While Revisiting Standards, National Research Council, Washington, DC, December 10-11, 2009. Available: http://www7.nationalacademies.org/bota/Mark_Wilson.pdf [accessed September 2010].

Wise, L. (2009). *How Common Standards Might Support Improved State Assessments.* Paper prepared for the workshop of the Committee on Best Practices for State Assessment Systems: Improving Assessment While Revisiting Standards, National Research Council, Washington, DC, December 10-11, 2009. Available: http://www7.nationalacademies.org/bota/Laurie_Wise_Paper.pdf [accessed September 2010].

Zwick, R. (2009). *State Achievement Comparisons: Is the Time Right?* Paper prepared for the workshop of the Committee on Best Practices for State Assessment Systems: Improving Assessment While Revisiting Standards, National Research Council, Washington, DC, December 10-11, 2009. Available: http://www7.nationalacademies.org/bota/Rebecca_Zwick_Paper.pdf [accessed September 2010].

Appendix A

Workshop Agendas

Best Practices for State Assessment Systems
Workshop 1
December 10-11, 2009

National Academy of Sciences
2100 C Street, NW
Washington, DC
Auditorium

Thursday, December 10

OPEN

9:15-9:45   **Welcome**
Stuart Elliott, Director, Board on Testing and Assessment
Judith Rizzo, Executive Director and CEO, James B. Hunt, Jr. Institute for Educational Leadership and Policy

Overview of Workshop Goals
Diana Pullin, *Chair,* Committee on Best Practices for State Assessment Systems

- **Précis of previous workshop series and report**
- **Overview of the goals and plans for the current workshop series**
- **Introduction of the idea of innovative assessment**
- **Discussion of the current status of the common standards movement**

9:45-11:30   **Session I. Examining the Status Quo: What Are the Benefits and Limitations of the Current Approaches to Assessment in This Country?**
Moderators: Diana Pullin, Dirk Mattson

(9:45-10:15) Overview of Current Assessment Practices
This session will provide a review of the current test-based accountability system, the goals and purposes it has developed to serve, and its strengths and limitations.
Presenter: Margaret Goertz, University of Pennsylvania

(10:15-10:45) Changes in Assessments and Assessment Systems Over the Past Decade
This session will review the ways assessments and approaches to assessment have changed over the past decade, including changes in item types, uses of local and interim assessments, and advancements in assessment of special populations.
Presenter: Scott Marion, National Center for Improvement of Educational Assessment (NCIEA)

(10:45-11:15) Synthesis of Key Ideas
Discussant: Joan Herman, National Center for Research on Evaluation, Standards, & Student Testing (CRESST)

(11:15-11:30) Focused Discussion
Moderators lead focused discussion with presenters and audience members.

11:30-12:15   **Working Lunch**

12:15-3:45   **Session II. Changing the Status Quo**
              Moderators: Joan Herman, Rebecca Maynard

(12:15-1:00) Developing Standards That Lead to Better Instruction and Learning
This session will discuss ways to specify standards so that they (1) more accurately delineate the skills and knowledge to be learned and (2) can be more accurately and readily translated into instruction and assessment. Examples will be drawn from the draft common core standards.
Presenters: Joe Krajcik and Shawn Stevens, University of Michigan

(1:00-1:45) Developing Assessment Tasks That Lead to Better Instruction and Learning
This session will explore ways to use more elaborated standards to develop assessment tasks that accurately measure the intended

skill and knowledge, with a particular focus on ways to ensure that assessments measure higher-order, critical thinking skills using a variety of item types.
Presenter: Mark Wilson, University of California, Berkeley

(1:45-2:30) Technical Challenges of Implementing Innovative Assessments
This session will explore the technical challenges associated with developing more innovative assessment tasks that measure challenging content and skills, tradeoffs associated with these kinds of assessments/tasks, and ways that the information gathered from innovative assessments might be used to support better decision making about students and instruction.
Presenter: Stephen Lazer, Educational Testing Service (ETS)

2:30-2:45 **Break**

2:45-3:15 **Synthesis of Key Ideas**
Discussant: Scott Marion, NCIEA

3:15-3:45 **Focused Discussion**
Moderators lead focused discussion with presenters and audience members.

3:45-5:00 **Session III.A What Is the Status of Innovative Assessment?**
Moderators: Diana Pullin, Mark Wilson

(3:45-4:30) Lessons from the Past and Current Efforts
This session will provide an overview of the experiences of pioneers in the area of innovative assessment, such as programs developed for Kentucky (KIRIS), Maryland (MSPAP), Vermont (Portfolio Assessment Program), and California (CLAS performance assessment) which are no longer in operation. Examples from currently operational assessment programs, international assessments, and in fields other than K-12 education will also be discussed.
Presenters: Brian Stecher and Laura Hamilton, RAND

(4:30-5:00) Focused Discussion
Moderators lead focused discussion with presenters and audience members.

5:00   Presentation by Lauren Resnick, Learning Research and
          Development Center, University of Pittsburgh

5:30   Adjourn Workshop
          Reception

6:00   Working Group Dinner (in Lecture Room)

Friday, December 11

OPEN

8:30-10:30   Session III.B What Is the Status of Innovative Assessment?
             (cont.)
             Moderators: Diana Pullin, Mark Wilson

(8:30-9:30) Panel Discussion: Political Considerations
This session will explore the political/practitioner perspective on
the pioneer program discussed in Part A. Panelists representing
several of the programs will address the following questions:

- What was the motivation for the assessment? Why was it
  considered? Who wanted it? Who wasn't in favor of it?
- What was involved in getting the assessment adopted?
  What, if any, obstacles were encountered? How were they
  overcome?
- What was involved in developing the assessment? What,
  if any, obstacles were encountered? How were they
  overcome?
- What issues were encountered with implementation of the
  assessment? What, if any, obstacles were encountered?
  How were they overcome?
- What were primary reasons for the demise of the
  program?

Panelists: Steve Ferrara (MSPAP), Brian Gong (KIRIS), and
Dirk Mattson (Minnesota)

(9:30-10:00) Synthesis of Key Ideas
Discussant: Lorraine McDonnell, University of California, Santa
Barbara

(10:00-10:30) Focused Discussion
Moderators lead focused discussion with presenters and audience members.

10:30-10:45   Break

10:45-2:30   Session IV. Exploring the Opportunities
Moderators: Rebecca Maynard, Dirk Mattson

(10:45-11:30) What Opportunities Does the Common Standards Movement Offer for Improving Assessment?
This session will explore the opportunities the common standards movement might offer for moving to more innovative assessments that assess challenging content and also give more information to teachers and local decision makers. The presentation will address technical issues and potential benefits of collaboration across states, drawing on examples from the experiences of Vermont, New Hampshire, Rhode Island, and Maine (New England Common Assessment Program)
Presenter: Laurie Wise, HumRRO

11:30-12:30   Working Lunch

12:30-2:15   Session IV. Exploring the Opportunities (cont.)

(12:30-1:15) Using Common Standards to Enable Cross-State Comparisons
This session will focus on the elements that would need to be in place in order for test results to be compared across states, including issues associated with adding state-specific items. The presentation will address the inferences that policy makers and test users might want to make and what is required to support each kind of inference.
Presenter: Ron Hambleton, University of Massachusetts, Amherst

(1:15-1:45) Synthesis of Key Ideas
Discussant: Rebecca Zwick, ETS and University of California, Santa Barbara

(1:45-2:15) Focused Discussion
Moderators lead focused discussion with presenters and audience members.

2:15-2:30   **Break**

2:30-4:00   **Session V. Setting Research Priorities**
                 Moderators: Diana Pullin, Scott Marion

                 (2:30-3:00) Research Priorities
                 The U.S. Department of Education has set aside $350 million
                 for developing tests to measure common standards. This
                 panel will listen to the workshop discussions and consider the
                 implications for research. The presenter and discussants will
                 address the following questions:

                 - Given the issues raised during the workshop, what are
                   realistic priorities for research?
                 - What projects/efforts are most in need of research?
                 - How would you proportionally allocate the funding?

                 Presenter: Lorrie Shepard, University of Colorado

                 (3:00-3:45) Responses
                 Discussants: Laurie Wise, HumRRO; Joan Herman, CRESST;
                 Rebecca Maynard, University of Pennsylvania

                 (3:45-4:15) Focused Discussion
                 Moderators lead focused discussion with presenters and
                 audience members.

4:15   **Closing Remarks, Adjourn**
                 Diana Pullin, *Chair*

Best Practices For State Assessment Systems
Workshop 2
April 6-7, 2010

National Academy of Sciences
2100 C Street, NW
Washington, DC
Auditorium

Tuesday, April 6

CLOSED

8:00   **Working breakfast for committee**
Discussion of agenda

8:30   **Discussion of plans for the workshop and moderator**
assignments

9:00   **Break to transition to open session**

OPEN

8:45-9:00   **Guests arrive, register**

9:15-9:45   **Opening Remarks**
- Stuart Elliott, Director, Board on Testing and Assessment
- Judith Rizzo, Executive Director and CEO, James B. Hunt Jr. Institute for Educational Leadership and Policy

            (9:30) Goals for the Workshop
- Diana Pullin, Boston College, Workshop Steering Committee Chair

9:45-2:45   **Session I. Developing Coherent Systems, Implementing**
Innovative Assessments
Issues to Discuss
- What does it mean to have a coherent system of assessments, with vertical, horizontal, and developmental coherence? Why is a coherent system important? What advantages does it offer?

- What are the different purposes of assessment and what assessment strategies best suit each purpose? How can the information provided by different forms of assessment be used to guide instruction, improve student learning, and evaluate effectiveness of teachers and schools for accountability purposes?
- What is involved in moving to a coherent system of assessment that incorporates multiple assessment types? What examples of such systems exist (nationally and internationally)?
- How can assessment of higher level thinking skills and deeper understandings be incorporated into a coherent system of assessments? What examples are currently being tried or considered?

(9:45-10:30) Coherent System of Assessments

Moderators:
Diana Pullin
Rebecca Maynard, University of Pennsylvania, Workshop Steering Committee

Presenter: Joan Herman, CRESST, Workshop Steering Committee

(10:30-10:45) Break

(10:45-11:30) Moderated Discussion: Policy Perspective

Panelists:
Roy Romer, College Board
Ed Roeber, Michigan State University

(11:30-12:00) Audience Discussion

12:00-1:00   Working Lunch

1:00-2:30   Reconvene to Continue Session I

(1:00-2:00) Moderated Discussion: Research and Practice Perspective

Moderators:
Diana Pullin
Dirk Mattson, Minnesota Department of Education

Panelists:
Linda Darling-Hammond, Stanford
Tony Alpert, Oregon Department of Education
Marc Tucker, National Center for Education and the Economy

(2:00-2:30) Audience Discussion

2:30-2:45   **Break**

2:45-5:00   **Session II. Issues to Consider with Innovative Assessments**

Issues to Address
- Innovative assessments pose challenges with respect to item development, administration, scoring, equating, and other technical issues. What are these challenges and how can they be addressed? How can we ensure that scores obtained from innovative assessments are reliable and valid?
- What issues need to be considered in using innovative assessment approaches with special populations?
- How can we ensure that these students have the opportunity to learn the material/skills needed for assessments that measure deeper understandings and higher order thinking skills?

(2:45-3:15) Ensuring That Innovative Assessments Provide Reliable and Valid Information

Moderators:
Scott Marion, National Center for Improvement of Educational Assessment, Workshop Steering Committee
Mark Wilson, UC Berkeley, Workshop Steering Committee

Presenter: Rebecca Zwick, UC Santa Barbara and ETS

(3:15-4:00) Moderated Discussion: Special Populations Perspectives

Panelists:
Robert Linquanti, West Ed
Martha Thurlow, National Center on Education Outcomes

(4:00-4:45) Moderated Discussion: Policy and Practice Perspective

Panelists:
Joe Willhoft, Washington Department of Education
Deborah Sigman, California Department of Education

(4:45-5:00) Audience Discussion

5:00-5:15   **Closing Remarks for Day 1**
               Gene Wilhoit, Council of Chief State School Officers
               Diana Pullin

5:15   **End of Formal Agenda for Day 1**
               Reception

6:00   **Working Group Dinner (in Lecture Room and Great Hall)**

Wednesday, April 7

8:30-11:45   **Session III. Strategies for Using Results from a Coherent System to Inform Instructional Decision Making**

               Issues to Address
               • How can assessment best be used to guide instruction?
               • What changes can be made to content standards, assessment tasks, and reports of assessment results to make them more useful for instruction?
               • What role can innovative assessment approaches play in guiding instruction?
               • What structures and supports need to be in place? What training do teachers need in order to effectively use assessment information?

(8:30-9:15) Strategies for Using Assessment to Guide Instruction

Moderators:
Joan Herman
Mark Wilson

Presenter: Linda Darling-Hammond, Stanford

(9:15-10:15) Moderated Discussion: Researcher Perspective

Panelists:
Margaret Heritage, CRESST
Karin Hess, National Center for the Improvement of Educational Assessment

10:15-10:30   Break

(10:30-11:15) Moderated Discussion: Policy Maker, Practitioner Perspectives

Panelists:
Teri Siskind, South Carolina Department of Education
Peg Cagle, LA Unified School District, California Teachers Advisory Council

(11:15-11:45) Audience Discussion

11:45-12:45   Working Lunch

12:45-2:15   Session IV: The Role of Technology

- What role can technology play in the implementation of innovative assessment strategies?
- What role can technology play in the scoring and reporting of innovative assessments?
- What role can technology play in making assessments and assessment results more useful for instruction?

(12:45-1:15) Technology and Innovative Assessment

Moderators:
Rebecca Maynard
Dirk Mattson

Presenter: Randy Bennett, ETS

(1:15-2:00) Policy maker, Practitioner Perspective

Panelists:
Wendy Pickett, Delaware Department of Education
Tony Alpert, Oregon Department of Education

(2:00-2:15) Audience Discussion

2:15-2:30   **Break**

2:30-4:00   **Session V. Synthesis and Extension of Ideas**

(2:30-3:15) Aggregating Information from Different Sources

Moderators:
Diana Pullin
Scott Marion

Presenter: Laurie Wise, HumRRO

The concept of "through-course" or "distributed summative assessment components" (e.g., assessment evidence collected over multiple points of time) has been discussed at several of the U.S. Department of Education-sponsored assessment hearings. This presentation will discuss how multiple types of assessment evidence can be used and aggregated to inform summative judgments. The presentation will address using aggregated information to evaluate students, teachers, and schools.

(3:15-4:00) Moderated Discussion with full steering committee

4:00   **Closing Remarks**
Diana Pullin

4:15   **Adjourn**

Appendix B

Workshop Participants

**PARTICIPANTS IN THE NATIONAL RESEARCH COUNCIL'S
WORKSHOP I ON BEST PRACTICES FOR
STATE ASSESSMENT SYSTEMS**

Joan Abdallah, American Association for the Advancement of Science
David Abrams, New York State Education Department
Frank Adamson, Stanford University
Martha Aliaga, American Statistical Association
Jaime Allentuck, Government Accounting Office
Guy-Alain Amoussou, National Science Foundation
Allison Armour-Garb, Rockefeller Institute of Government
Sally Atkins-Burnett, Mathematica
Margaret Bartz, Chicago Public Schools
Alix Beatty, National Research Council
Rolf K. Blank, Council of Chief State School Officers
Molly Broad, American Council on Education
Gina Broxterman, National Center for Education Statistics
JB Buxton, Metametrics
Peg Cagle, California Teacher Advisory Council
Micheline Chalhoub-Deville, University of North Carolina, Greensboro
Doug Christensen, Nebraska Department of Education
Julia Clark, National Science Foundation
Sherri Coles, Family Support Center on Disabilities
Bruce W. Colletti, Northern Virginia Community College
Jere Confrey, North Carolina State University

Tim Crockett, Measured Progress
Christopher Cross, Cross and Joftus, LLC
Jerome Dancis, University of Maryland
Linda Darling-Hammond, Stanford University
Stephanie Dean, James B. Hunt, Jr. Institute
George E. DeBoer, American Association for the Advancement of Science
Gabriel Della-Piana, University of Utah
Betty Demarest, National Education Association Research
Craig Deville, Measurement Incorporated
Pasquale DeVito, Measured Progress
Shelby Dietz, Center on Education Policy
Chris Domalski, National Center for the Improvement of Educational
    Assessment
Nancy Doorey, Educational Testing Service
Kelly Duncan, National Research Council
Janice Earle, National Science Foundation
John Easton, U.S. Department of Education
Tracey Edou, U.S. Department of Energy
David Egnor, U.S. Department of Education
Lisa Ehrlich, Measured Progress
Stuart Elliott, National Research Council
John Ewing, Math for America
Florence D. Fasanelli, American Association for the Advancement of Science
Steve Ferrara, CTB/McGraw-Hill
Michael Feuer, National Research Council
Rebecca Fitch, U.S. Office for Civil Rights
Beth Foley, National Education Association
Pat Forgione, Educational Testing Service
Denise Forte, U.S. House of Representatives, Committee on Education and
    Labor
Gavin Fulmer, National Science Foundation
Randall Garton, Shanker Institute
Michael Gilligan, James B. Hunt, Jr. Institute
Alan Ginsburg, U.S. Department of Education
Margaret Goertz, University of Pennsylvania
Brian Gong, National Center for Improvement of Educational Assessment
Mandi Gordon, George Mason University
Mark D. Greenman, National Science Foundation
Eunice Greer, National Center for Education Statistics
Laura Hamilton, RAND
Pierce Hammond, Office of Vocational and Adult Education
Mariana Haynes, National Association of State Boards of Education
Andres Henriquez, The Carnegie Corporation

Joan Herman, National Center for Research on Evaluation, Standards, and
    Student Testing (committee member)
Richard Hill, National Science Foundation
Margaret Hilton, National Research Council
Gene Hoffman, Human Resources Research Organization
Yung-chen Hsu, American Council on Education
Bruce Hunter, American Association of School Administrators
Kirk Janowiak, U.S. Department of Education
Arundhati Jayarao, Einstein Fellow, Office of Senator Kirsten Gillibrand
    (D-NY)
Michael Jennings, University of Alabama
Wyn Jennings, National Science Foundation
Allan Jones, Emaginos
Barb Kapinus, National Education Association
Martin Kehe, GED Testing Service
Tom Keller, National Research Council
William Kelly, American Society for Engineering Education
Eugenia Kemble, Shanker Institute
Julie Kochanek, Learning Point Associates
Judith Koenig, National Research Council
Ken Krehbiel, National Council of Teachers of Mathematics
Melissa Lazarin, Center for American Progress
Steve Lazer, Educational Testing Service
Anne Lewis, K-12 Assessment and Performance Management Center,
    Educational Testing Service
Dane Linn, National Governors Association
Alan Maloney, NC State University
David Mandel, National Center on Education and the Economy
Scott Marion, National Center for the Improvement of Educational Assessment
    (committee member)
Dirk Mattson, Minnesota Department of Education (committee member)
Rebecca Maynard, University of Pennsylvania (committee member)
Lorraine McDonnell, University of California, Santa Barbara
Jamie McKee, Bill & Melinda Gates Foundation
Tiah McKinney, George Mason University
Raegen Miller, Center for American Progress
Sherri Miller, ACT, Inc.
Zipporah Miller, National Science Teachers Association
Chris Minnich, Council of Chief State School Officers
Hassan Minor, Howard University Middle School of Mathematics and Science
William Montague, Association of Independent Schools of Greater Washington
Scott Montgomery, Council of Chief State School Officers
Jean Moon, National Research Council

Patricia Morison, National Research Council
Lesley Muldoon, Achieve
F. Howard Nelson, AFL-CIO
Rose Neugroschel, National Research Council
Alexander Nicholas, National Science Foundation
Steven Obenhaus, Office of Senator Joseph I. Lieberman (ID-CT)
Carol O'Donnell, U.S. Department of Education
Cornelia Orr, National Assessment Governing Board
Ray Pecheone, Stanford University
Anthonette Pena, National Science Foundation
Marianne Perie, National Center for the Improvement of Educational
    Assessment
Ashley Clark Perry, James B. Hunt, Jr. Institute
Kristina Peterson, House Committee on Education and Labor
Valena Plisko, National Center for Education Statistics
Gerrita Postlewait, Stupski Foundation
Diana Pullin, Boston College (committee chair)
Sam Rankin, American Mathematical Society
Joseph Reed, National Science Foundation
Sue Rigney, U.S. Department of Education
Judith Rizzo, James B. Hunt, Jr. Institute
Roy Romer, The College Board
Robert Rothman, Alliance for Excellent Education
Gerhard Salinger, National Science Foundation
Eugene Schaffer, University of Maryland, Baltimore
Elizabeth Schneider, Alliance for Excellent Education
Susan Sclafani, National Center for Education and the Economy
Kelly Scott, The Aspen Institute-Commission on NCLB
Robert Scott, Texas Department of Education
Barbara Shannon, California Teachers Advisory Council
Lorri Shepard, University of Colorado
Elena Silva, Education Sector
Malbert Smith, MetaMetrics
Patty Sobecky, University of Alabama
Nancy Spillane, National Science Foundation
Brian Stecher, RAND
Jack Stenner, MetaMetrics
Marc Sternberg, U.S. Department of Education
Shawn Stevens, University of Michigan
Justin Stone, Associate for the American Federation of Teachers
Martin Storksdieck, National Research Council
Bonnie Bracey Sutton, Emaginos
Vic Sutton, Emaginos

Kevin Sweeney, The College Board
Monica Thammarath, Southeast Asia Resource Action Center
Doua Thor, Southeast Asia Resource Action Center
Tom Toch, Association of Independent Schools of Greater Washington
LeRoy Tompkins, Office of the State Superintendent of Education, DC
Elizabeth VanderPutten, National Science Foundation
Dave Vannier, National Institutes for Health
Joyce VanTassel-Baska, Center for Gifted Education
David Wakelyn, National Governors Association
Michael Wallace, Howard University
Wanda Ward, Education and Human Resources, National Science Foundation
Denny Way, Pearson
Susan Weigert, U.S. Department of Education
Joanne Weiss, U.S. Department of Education, Race to the Top Initiative
Antoinette Wells, National Aeronautics and Space Administration Education Program
Ann Whalen, U.S. Department of Education
April White, James B. Hunt, Jr. Institute
Amber Wilke, Northwest Evaluation Association
Joe Willhoft, Office of Superintendent of Public Instruction, Washington
Mark Wilson, University of California, Berkeley (committee member)
Bob Wise, Alliance for Excellent Education
Lauress Wise, Human Resources Research Organization
Steve Wise, Northwest Evaluation Association
Zhijian Wu, University of Alabama
Judy Wurtzel, U.S. Department of Education, Office of Planning, Evaluation and Policy Development
Raymond Yeagley, Northwest Evaluation Association
Rebecca Zwick, University of California, Santa Barbara, and Educational Testing Service

PARTICIPANTS IN THE NATIONAL RESEARCH COUNCIL'S WORKSHOP II ON BEST PRACTICES FOR STATE ASSESSMENT SYSTEMS

Diane Adger-Johnson, Office of Special Populations and Research Training, DEA
Maya Agarwal, Carnegie Corporation of New York
Eileen Ahearn, National Association for State Directors of Special Education
Manuel Alfero, American Institutes for Research
Tony Alpert, Oregon Department of Education
Joseph Amenta, Connecticut State Department of Education
Gilbert Andrada, Connecticut Department of Education

William Auty, Education Measurement Consulting
Peggy Baker, EASL Institute
Doug Baldwin, Educational Testing Service
Charles Barone, Democrats for Education Reform
Tyrana Battle, North Carolina Department of Public Instruction
Alix Beatty, National Research Council
Rolf Blank, Council of Chief State School Officers
Toni Bowen, GA DOE/Division for Exceptional Students
Peg Cagle, California Teachers Advisory Council
Andy Calkins, Stupski Foundation
Marti Canipe, National Science Foundation
Stephanie Carlos, Louisiana Department of Education
Wendy Carver, Utah State Office of Education
Christi Chadwick, North Carolina Department of Public Instruction
Matt Chapman, Northwest Evaluation Association
Anne Chartrand, Southeast Regional Resource Center
David Chayer, Data Recognition Corporation
Fen Chou, Louisiana Department of Education
Beth Cipoletti, West Virginia Department of Education
Tom Collins, Wyoming Department of Education
Jere Confrey, Friday Institute for Educational Innovation College of
    Education, North Carolina State University
Sidney Cooley, Kansas State Department of Education
Christopher Cross, Cross and Joftus, LLC
Stan Curtis, Tennessee Department of Education
Linda Darling-Hammond, Stanford University
Lucille Davy, James B. Hunt, Jr. Institute
Stephanie Dean, James B. Hunt, Jr. Institute
Thomas Deeter, Iowa Department of Education
Gabriel Della-Piana, Consultant on program design, development, research,
    and evaluation
Pasquale DeVito, Measured Progress
Mohamed Dirir, Connecticut Department of Education
Richard Dobbs, Large Scale Business Development
Nancy Doorey, Center for K-12 Assessment and Performance Management
Karen Douglas, Institute of Education Sciences
Ken Draut, Kentucky Department of Education
Janice Earle, National Science Foundation
Emerson Elliott, National Council for Accreditation for Teacher Education
Stuart Elliott, National Research Council
Steve Enck, SAS Institute
Kevin Fangman, Iowa Department of Education
Aran Felix, Alaska Department of Education and Early Development

Wanda Fields, American Council on Education
Rebecca Fitch, Office for Civil Rights/U.S. Department of Education
Mary Fowles, Educational Testing Service
Gavin Fulmer, National Science Foundation
Otis Fulton, MetaMetrics, Inc.
Elizabeth Fultz, Kansas State Department of Education
Ashley Gardiner, Council of Chief State School Officers
Catherine Gewertz, Education Week
Stella Gibbs, Pacific Metrics
Michael Gilligan, James B. Hunt, Jr. Institute
Imelda Go, South Carolina Department of Education
Mandi Gordon, George Mason University
Cindy Greer, Kentucky Department of Education
Tracy Halka, Achieve
Shiqi Hao, Michigan Department of Education
David Happe, Iowa Department of Education
Dianne Henderson-Montero, Educational Testing Service
Sara Hennings, MetaMetrics, Inc.
Andrés Henríquez, Carnegie Corporation of New York
Margaret Heritage, National Center for Research on Evaluation, Standards, and Student Testing
Joan Herman, National Center for Research on Evaluation, Standards, and Student Testing (committee member)
Karin Hess, National Center for the Improvement of Educational Assessment
Margaret Hilton, National Research Council
Kirk Janowiak, U.S. Department of Energy
Arundhati Jayarao, Office of Senator Kirsten E. Gillibrand (NY)
Elizabeth Jehangiri, South Dakota Department of Education
Joanne Jensen, WestEd
Elizabeth Jones, South Carolina Department of Education
Barb Kapinus, National Education Association
Thomas Keller, National Research Council
Anthony (Eamonn) Kelly, College of Education and Human Development, George Mason University
Dana Kelly, National Center for Education Statistics
Judy Koenig, National Research Council
Jim Kohlmoos, Knowledge Alliance
Laura Kramer, Mississippi Department of Education
Ken Krehbiel, National Council of Teachers of Mathematics
Caroline Lang, Department of Defense Education Activity
Sheryl Lazarus, National Center on Educational Outcomes
Robert Linquanti, WestEd
Miriam Lund, U.S. Department of Education

Duncan MacQuarrie, Council of Chief State School Officers
Paula Mahaley, Ohio Department of Education
Alan Maloney, Friday Institute for Educational Innovation College of
    Education North Carolina State University
David Mandel, National Center on Education and the Economy
Scott Marion, National Center for Improvement of Educational Assessment
    (committee member)
Deborah Matthews, Kansas State Department of Education
Dirk Mattson, Minnesota Department of Education (committee member)
Rebecca Maynard, University of Pennsylvania (committee member)
James McBride, Renaissance Learning
Nadine McBride, North Carolina Department of Public Instruction
Jim McCann, American Institutes for Research
Daniel McGrath, National Center for Education Statistics
Jamie McKee, Bill & Melinda Gates Foundation
Marlene Metts, South Carolina Department of Education
George Michna, Connecticut State Department of Education
Sherri Miller, ACT, Inc.
Carissa Miller, Idaho State Department of Education
Jeanine Molock, Ohio Department of Education
Mira Monroe, Colorado Department of Education
Alan Moore, Wyoming Department of Education
Patricia Morison, National Research Council
Anthony Moss, Kansas Department of Education
Howard Nelson, American Federation of Teachers, AFL-CIO
Paul Nichols, Pearson
Shilpi Niyogi, Pearson
Steven Obenhaus, Senator Joseph I. Lieberman (ID-CT)
Paula O'Gorman, Renaissance Learning
Marie O'Hara, Achieve
John Olson, Olson Educational Measurement & Assessment Services
Cornelia Orr, National Assessment Governing Board
Eugene Owen, National Center for Education Statistics
James Palmer, Illinois State Board of Education
Marianne Perie, Center for Assessment
Ashley Clark Perry, James B. Hunt, Jr. Institute
Gary Phillips, American Institutes for Research
Nick Pinchok, Learning Point Associates
Val Plisko, National Center for Education Statistics
Diana Pullin, Boston College (committee chair)
Cherie Randall, Kansas State Department of Education
Sue Rigney, U.S. Department of Education
Douglas Rindone, Council of Chief State School Officers

Judith Rizzo, James B. Hunt, Jr. Institute
Ed Roeber, Michigan State University
Roy Romer, The College Board
Pat Roschewski, Nebraska Department of Education
Robert Rothman, Alliance for Excellent Education
Lynette Russell, Wisconsin Department of Public Instruction
Sharon Sáez, Council of Chief State School Officers
Edynn Sato, WestEd
Mark Saul, Education Development Center Inc.
Sheila Schultz, Human Resources Research Organization
Caroline Seabrook, Educational Value-Added Assessment System
Kris Shaw, Kansas State Department of Education
Alan Sheinker, State Solutions, Council of Chief State School Officers
Marc Siciliano, Teaching Institute for Excellence in STEM
Deborah Sigman, California Department of Education
Rhonda Sims, Education, Assessment and Accountability
Norma Sinclair, Connecticut State Department of Education
Theresa Siskind, South Carolina Department of Education
Sharon Slater, Educational Testing Service
Larry Snowhite, McGraw-Hill Education
Thomas Spencer, Louisiana Department of Education
Marc Sternberg, U.S. Department of Education
Wendy McLaughlin Stoica, Ohio Department of Education
Justin Stone, American Federation of Teachers
Janet Stuck, Connecticut State Department of Education
Suzanne Swaffield, South Carolina Department of Education
Kevin Sweeney, The College Board
Melinda Taylor, North Carolina Department of Public Instruction
Rebecca Thessin, Harvard University
Charles Thomas, George Mason University
Martha Thurlow, National Center on Education Outcomes
Bill Tucker, Innovative Ideas
Marc Tucker, National Center for Education and the Economy
Linda Turner, South Dakota Department of Education
Benecia Tuthill, Department of Defense Education Activity
Jess Unger, American Institutes for Research
Dave Vannier, National Institutes of Health
Steven Viger, Michigan Department of Education
Jim Walker
Sandra Warren, Council of Chief State School Officers
Heath Weems, Educational Testing Service
Susan Weigert, U.S. Department of Education
Joanne Weiss, U.S. Department of Education

John Weiss, Pennsylvania Department of Education
Antoinette Wells, National Aeronautics and Space Administration Education
    Program
Ann Whalen, U.S. Department of Education
Gene Wilhoit, Council of Chief State School Officers
Joseph Willhoft, Office of Superintendent of Public Instruction
Leila Williams, Arizona Department of Education
Mark Wilson, University of California, Berkeley (committee member)
Phoebe Winter, Pacific Metrics
Laurie Wise, Human Resources Research Organization
Steven Wise, Northwest Evaluation Association
Judy Wurtzel, Office of Planning, Evaluation and Policy Development
Holly Xie, National Center for Education Statistics
Dengke Xu, Ohio Department of Education
Raymond Yeagley, Northwest Evaluation Association
Shu Jing Yen, Institute of Education Sciences
Ray Young, Pennsylvania Department of Education
Dalia Zabala, American Federation of Teachers
Molly Zebrowski, Riverside Publishing
Liru Zhang, Delaware Department of Education
Rebecca Zwick, University of California, Santa Barbara and Educational
    Testing Service